MICHAEL WYNNE

Canvas

faber and faber

First published in 2012
by Faber and Faber Limited
74–77 Great Russell Street
London WC1B 3DA

Typeset by Country Setting, Kingsdown, Kent CT14 8ES
Printed in England by CPI Group (UK) Ltd, Croydon CR0 4YY

A CIP record for this book
is available from the British Library

ISBN 978-0-571-29599-9

2 4 6 8 10 9 7 5 3 1

Canvas was first performed in the Minerva Theatre, Chichester, on 18 May 2012. The cast was as follows:

Bridget Sarah Hadland
Alan Dean Lennox Kelly
Amanda Hattie Ladbury
Rory Elliot Levey
Alistair Oliver Milburn
Justine Lucy Montgomery
Bronwyn Lisa Palfrey

Director Angus Jackson
Designer Jonathan Fensom
Lighting Designer Mark Howland
Music Grant Olding
Sound Designer Gareth Fry
Casting Director Alastair Coomer

Characters

Justine
Alan

Mia
Thomas
their children

Bridget
Rory

Amanda
Alistair

Camilla
their daughter

Bronwyn

This text went to press before the end of rehearsals,
so may differ slightly from the play as performed.

CANVAS

Act One

SCENE ONE

A large tent in the middle of a field. More like a mini-house than a tent. All brown canvas with plastic windows on the front and a pitched roof. The tent is on a diagonal with the entrance to one side. Three wooden steps lead to the closed tent flaps. A large tree behind, the branches reaching out over the roof. A dry stone wall behind. There are two other identical tents in the field to the left and right that we can't see. The right-hand side leads to a gate and farmhouse.

It's early evening and the sun is going down behind the tent. There's a lovely red glow and it looks very appealing.

Justine appears from the right carrying her sleeping daughter, Mia, five, who's gripping a battered-looking pink teddy, even though she's fast asleep.

Justine (*to Alan behind her*) Leave the bags. And you don't need to lock it, there's no one else about. (*She comes to the tent.*) It must be this one. (*She looks out at the view, taking it all in. Lifting Mia up slightly to hold her more comfortably.*) Look at that view. (*Half to herself.*) It's beautiful.

Justine takes it in for a moment. A moment of peace. Alan appears carrying a sleeping son, Thomas, six.

Alan The middle one, she said the middle one.

Justine Shush. It must be this tent. There's someone in that one.

Alan looks out as he joins her.

Alan Wow, look at that. We're on top of the lake.

3

Justine tries to pull at various flaps on the front – she can't work out how to get inside.

Justine How the hell do you . . .?

Alan pulls back a small flap and sees the entrance tied up.

Alan It's all knotted together like an old scout tent.

He moves to open it, but it's awkward while he's carrying Thomas.

It's a bit tricky with . . . I could put him back in the car.

Justine Gimme.

Justine holds out her free arm and Alan passes her Thomas. She holds both children, one in each arm. It's some weight.

Oh my God.

Alan Now, is it tied at the top or bottom?

Justine Can we just get in before my spine collapses? They weigh a ton.

Alan I see . . .

He starts untying the loops from the bottom. Mia moans and moves about, like she's waking up.

Justine Shush now.

Alan We could let them wake up.

Justine It's well past their bedtime.

Alan I'm sure they'd love to see it here.

Justine They can see it in the morning. Just . . .

Alan Getting there.

Justine I can feel each vertebra snapping.

Alan I told you we should have set off earlier. When we went on holiday as kids we'd get up really early, half asleep, almost the middle of the night. We'd get there and still have a whole day to play.

Justine You and your perfect holidays. I can't hold them much longer.

Mia moves again and drops the teddy, Sheila, into a muddy puddle.

Right in a puddle. Oh great.

Alan takes the teddy out of the mud.

She's half covered in sick anyway. I've never seen a child produce so much vomit. Those bendy roads. It was like we were re-enacting *The Exorcist*.

Justine holds out a hand. Alan passes the teddy.
He gets back to opening the tent.
Adult laughter comes from Alistair and Amanda in the tent on the left.

(*Looking across.*) Did you hear that? I forgot you can hear everything when you're camping.

Alan That's one of the joys.

Alan stops untying and looks over.

Justine How is that a joy? Don't stop what you're doing.

Alan undoes the knots halfway so they can get in. He pulls it back to let Justine inside.

At last.

Justine hands him Thomas and goes inside with Mia and Sheila.
We now see the inside of the tent – either through the walls disappearing, a revolve, or some other trick. It's a square room with a floor of old wooden

floorboards. There's a wood-burner with a small stove on top in the middle. A sink and work surface next to it. An old Welsh dresser with crockery and pans behind. Retro tins filled with cutlery and utensils. An old wooden table with a variety of second-hand chairs around it. A welcome basket on the table. A large wooden box on the floor which acts as a coolbox. An oil lamp and candle-holders hanging up. Behind the dresser is a passage which leads through to the beds. A curtain separating the two parts of the tent. It all looks very home-made and inviting.

Justine stands in the middle of the room holding Mia and taking it all in for a moment. Alan joins her with Thomas.

Alan Now look at this. This is our new home.

Justine drifts off for a moment. She heads off.

Justine The beds must be . . .

She chucks Sheila in the sink as she passes and heads off through the passage.

Alan I love it. I think we're going to be really happy here. (*He looks round.*) Look at it.

Justine comes back out.

Justine I've put her in the top bunk. She'd kick off if she woke up in the bottom one. It's cosy in there. There's bunk beds on one side and a big double bed on the other.

Alan heads through.

Alan (*off*) I told you you'd like it once we got here.

Justine takes her coat off and throws it across a chair. She has a look round. She's impressed. At the wood-burner, looking inside the furnace. She finds the welcome pack in a wicker basket. She looks inside, taking out some candlesticks, tea lights, firelighters and a board game. There's a handwritten note: she tries to read but it's hard to decipher.

She sits down on one of the chairs to read the note but the back falls off. She manages to save herself before landing on the floor.

Alan comes back out.

Alan It's great. It's like . . . it's like camping but not, but with beds and stuff.

Justine They should put that on the advert. This chair's just died. Nearly arse over tit.

Alan It's all part of the look, isn't it? That shabby-chic thing.

Justine You just break your neck in the process. There's a welcome pack.

Alan That's nice of them.

He takes his coat off and throws it across the table.

Justine There's this handwritten note which I can't make head nor tail of. (*Reading from the paper.*) 'Hey . . . Canapés?'

She shows it to Alan.

Alan 'Campers'.

Justine 'Sorry I'm not there to greet you . . . I hope everything's . . .'

Alan 'Fine'.

Justine 'I'll be by later to cook . . . check in on you.' Was she blindfolded when she wrote this? 'There's a *something* of *something* and a welcome box and a basket of wool . . . wood . . . Any problems call me on o-seven . . .' Is that a three, six or an eight? Well, we won't be calling her. 'Blob . . .' What's her name?

7

Alan Bronwyn and Julian.

Justine (*turning the paper over*) There's a drawing here of . . . I don't know what.

Alan It's this tent. That's the sink there? And table? What does that say? 'Mouse'?

Justine There's a mouse?

Alan And look, she's drawn a picture of it too.

Justine (*looking round the floor*) A mouse? Oh, there isn't, is there? I'd jump on a chair but it'd fall apart.

Alan I think she's saying it lives behind here (*the coolbox*).

Justine Oh no. Can you see it?

Alan It'll be a cute little field mouse. The kids'll love it. I'd prefer a mouse to a rat.

Justine I don't want either of them. Oh my God, there it is.

She runs behind the work surface. Alan looks.

Alan Oh yeah. (*He bends down to pick it up.*)

Justine Just get rid of it. Don't pick it up.

Alan picks it up and moves towards Justine.

Have you got it? Have you got it? No, go away.

He opens his hands.

Alan Look.

Justine No, no . . . Oh, it's a sock. (*She looks at it.*) It's not one of ours.

Alan jumps the rolled-up sock along his arm making squeaking noises.

Alan Squeak, squeak.

Justine Is it a bit cold? I'm cold. Are you cold?

Alan Aren't you glad we've come?

Justine I don't know yet.

Bridget (*from the other tent on the right*) Oh Rory. Now what have I told you?

Justine Listen. I wonder what the others are like?

Alan They'll be just like us . . . Families with kids needing a holiday. I'll get the bags. We can bed down for the night, it's getting dark. Light the fire. Snuggle up.

Justine Okay, okay. I can do this. I've put some goodies in the cooler bag. A bottle of nice wine and some nibbles. I'll make it cosy.

Alan That's the spirit. (*He gives her a kiss.*) This is going to be great.

Justine Yeah. This is just what we need.

Alan heads out of the front flap and round to the right to the car.
  Justine has more of a look round. Wary of the coolbox and any mice that may be hiding nearby. She takes the basket of logs and sits down in front of the burner to light the fire. She crumples up some paper and places some small logs on top but is confused about the air vent. She doesn't get very far.
  Bridget and Rory appear from the right with washbags and towels over their arms. They are dressed appropriately for the outdoors.

Rory We can speak to them tomorrow.

Bridget It'll only take a minute. (*She knocks on the canvas flap.*) I tried to knock but it made no sound. Silly me.

Justine is slightly startled. Bridget pokes her head through the flap.

Bridget Hello?

Justine Oh, hello.

Bridget We just wanted to welcome you. Didn't we?

Rory Yes, yes, we did.

Justine That's nice. Ah, thanks.

Bridget Welcome.

Rory (*from behind her, quieter*) Welcome.

An awkward pause, as Bridget has just her head through the flap.

Justine Why don't you come . . .?

Bridget is in the tent before Justine has finished the sentence.

Bridget Are you sure?

Justine Doesn't feel right talking to a disembodied head.

Bridget I've got a full body attached, arms, legs, everything.

Justine Yes, I see.

Rory tries to sneak off. Bridget shakes hands.

Bridget I'm Bridget and this is . . . Rory. Rory? Come in.

Rory reluctantly enters.

Rory Hello.

Justine Hiya. I'm Justine.

Bridget We just wanted to welcome you. There's only us three tents. I thought there'd be more. But we're all in this together! And it's good to get to know each other, isn't it? It's so lovely. We love it. Do you love it?

Justine tidies away hers and Alan's coat.

Justine Yeah, it's great.

Rory Well, we're just next door. We'll let you settle in.

He moves to leave.

Bridget Is it just you then and the children? I take it you're here with children? I suppose you could come here without but why would you . . .

Justine Yes, I'm here with the kids and my husband.

Bridget Oh, for a minute I thought it was just you. A single parent. Which would have been great. And then I thought maybe you've come by yourself. Just you and the children. He's working hard back home, couldn't come or you've had a row and just thought. 'That's it, sod you, I'm taking them away on my own.' I had lots of thoughts in that moment.

Justine Right. He's getting the bags from the car.

Bridget Are your little ones asleep?

She pokes her head through the curtain to the kids.

Rory (*quiet*) I'm so sorry. She means well.

Justine It's fine.

Bridget (*coming back out*) Oh, look at them. They love the bunks, don't they? We've got two, so have Amanda and Alistair. On the other end. They'll love it tomorrow when they can all play together. Ours love games and play.

Rory It's all for the kids, isn't it? Family all together.

Justine I hope we get a break too. I'd offer you a drink but . . .

Rory We were just going to have a wash, passing by, we should probably leave you.

Justine Have you seen any mice? Apparently we've got one in here.

Bridget Ah, a little baby field mouse. Harmless enough. Do you want us to show you where everything is? How it all works?

Justine Don't worry.

Bridget The wood-burner's a bugger.

Rory A bugger.

Bridget We've mastered it. We can either show you or you'll be faffing about for hours. The choice is yours.

Rory I'll get the kindling ready.

Rory gets together small twigs and pieces of wood from the basket and scrunches up newspaper. Bridget crouches down at the burner.

Bridget Now concentrate. This is the ash pan. (*She pulls out a pan from the stove.*) We weren't sure what this was and put the firelighters in here at first. Silly billies. You need to empty this of ash every now and again. This second handle is to shake the grate to let the ash out and let more air in. (*She opens the burner door and lets out a gasp.*) Now who's had a go here? Done it all wrong. Was it you?

Justine It was already like that when I opened it.

Bridget Really?

Justine Alan, my husband, must have been him.

Bridget Well, he's on detention when he gets back. He's made the first fatal mistake. Putting the wood in flat. It's all about the . . .

Bridget and Rory both make a triangle shape with their two hands and looks to Justine.

Justine Triangle?

Bridget shakes her head.

Roof of house?

Rory makes a sand-dancer shape behind Bridget's back.

Bridget Don't help her. You can get it.

Justine Tent?

Rory (*in a cough*) Egypt.

Justine Pyramid?

Bridget That's cheating. We're going to have to deduct a point for cheating.

Justine Anyhow . . .

Bridget Ah yes. It's all about the . . . (*She makes the shape.*)

Justine Pyramid.

Bridget So air can circulate and fan the flames. If you put them flat on top of each other, like this, it all goes out. The same with the logs once we get this kindling going. Always . . .

All three of them make the shape.

Pyramids. You taking this all in?

Justine Yes, Miss.

Bridget So we build a small pyramid of paper and kindling. (*To Rory.*) Nurse?

Rory passes the paper and kindling. Bridget places the twigs and paper inside the burner.

Bridget Firelighters.

Rory Of course, Doctor.

He passes the firelighters.

Bridget We sprinkle these about. Get them right inside. Perfect. Matches, Nurse.

Rory strikes a large cook's match and passes it to Bridget.

Rory Yes, Doctor.

Bridget Thank you, Nurse.

Bridget lights firelighters and the paper. The kindling starts to light.

But now's the crucial time. Ready with extra twigs and smallish branches to get it going . . .

Justine You know, that's great . . .

Rory How about I show you how the oil lamp works?

Justine Oh no . . .

Rory I insist. You've got heat. You need light. It's a bit of a conundrum.

Rory starts working on the oil lamp.

Bridget It's going good now. A few smallish branches on.

Justine doesn't know what to do with herself.
  Alan comes back carrying many big bags.
  The wood-burning stove can be smelt.

Alan Here we are. (*He sees the busy scene.*) Oh, hello.

Rory lights the lamp.

Rory And then there was light.

Alan (*to Justine*) You getting to know everyone?

Justine Looks like it.

Alan I'm Alan.

He shakes hands with Rory.

Rory Rory and Bridget. We're just next door on the right.

Bridget Alistair and Amanda on your left. You piggy in the middle.

Alan Yeah.

Bridget Isn't it great? We love it. Do you love it?

Alan We've only just got here but, oh, yeah. It's great how they've done it all out.

Bridget (*about fire*) We'll leave that for a minute . . . What else?

Justine It's fine, please.

Rory (*to Alan*) First time camping? If you can call this camping.

Alan We've been the last couple of years with the kids. To this campsite I used to go to with my family when I was little. Over in Anglesey. The kids love camping. Justine hates it.

Justine No, I don't. You just never get a proper night's sleep. You need a holiday to recover from the holiday.

Alan So this is a compromise. Proper beds. And the farm and everything.

Rory We used to go every year, even when the children were tiny . . . but this is the first time in a while.

Bridget Yeah.

Rory But we're having a great time so far, aren't we?

Bridget We're getting on much better here than we have in *years*. At home. But it's only been a day so far.

Rory Reminds me that we can have a good time together. Our little family.

Bridget (*not getting drawn in*) This is looking good now.

Rory Camping tests anyone's resolve. But I love it. Always gone camping, ever since I was a kid. Every summer we'd go away for a whole month and no poncey campsites for my dad. You had to be at one with nature. Up some mountain, in the middle of nowhere, really feeling the elements. God, what he'd make of it here. He wouldn't approve. Beds, wood-burners, hot food. He'd be furious, if he wasn't *dead*. Other friends were going to exotic places where you had warmth and sunshine like Disney World or Spain. But we were much happier. Listening to the rain on the canvas. Trying not to touch the sides in case the water came through. Eating food out of a billycan like you were in World War One. And if we complained he'd beat us within an inch of our lives. Happy times.

Alan Okay, yeah. So . . .

Rory It's character-building. The children say they hate it, just like I hated it but they'll appreciate it when they're older. Like I think I do now. In fact we met on a campsite. I can remember the first words we said like they were yesterday. Bridge was coming out of the toilet block . . .

Bridget 'There's no paper left in this one.'

Rory 'It's okay, I only want a number one.'

Alan Right.

Justine Romantic.

Rory And we're on holiday and we're doing our bit for the environment too.

Bridget We're saving the planet while we're here.

Rory No long flights, it's all organic.

Bridget The other day I bought some non-organic milk and I just felt awful afterwards.

Rory You've got to think of the world we're leaving to our children.

Bridget We always say, think of the little dormouse. When you're going to buy something non-organic think of that dormouse and that you might be about to kill him stone dead.

Rory But we should let you settle in.

Bridget And you know, tough times, tough times. So . . .

Justine Tell us about it.

Bridget We're all finding it hard, had to cut back. We're lucky to get these tents. Everyone wants to go camping now.

Alan Well, we're here now. Let's make the most of it.

Bridget What are your plans for tomorrow? We could all do something together. I'm sure Alistair and Amanda would love it.

Alan We haven't got that far.

Bridget Maybe we could do a sports day? An educational one where we test the children on parts of the body and the local area.

Rory We'll let you settle in.

Bridget Let's speak in the morning and make plans. We're up six, seven. Just give us a knock.

Alan Maybe not at six.

Bridget See you in the morning. Bright and early. (*Looking into burner.*) Time for another . . . Remember the . . .

> *Bridget and Rory make the shape. Justine does it back. Alan is confused.*

Rory If you need anything just give us a shout.

Bridget Night, campers.

Rory Night.

Alan Bye.

Justine See you. And thanks again.

Bridget and Rory leave and head off to the right to the wash room.

I'll get the kids, you get the bags.

Alan They're not that bad. They're fun.

Justine You forgot the cooler bag.

Alan This is everything.

Justine No, there's the green cooler bag with all the . . .

Alan Have we already brought it in?

Justine No. Did you pick it up off the kitchen floor?

Alan Was I supposed to?

Justine Yes, I was taking the kids to the loo for the umpteenth time before we set off and I sent you back in to make sure we'd got all the bags.

Alan And I was meant to know there were bags in the kitchen as well as the bags in the hall?

Justine Well, it's implicit, isn't it? It means any bags that are in the house.

Alan So I should have checked every room to see if there were any bags hidden about? Like a weird secret treasure hunt that only you know about. Looking behind the sofa and under the sink.

Justine That's what I would have done.

Alan So we've got no cooler bag?

Justine No. So no wine, beer, cheese, bread. Those dark chocolates you like with the little . . .

Alan You're adding things that weren't even in it now. Have we got any food or drink?

Justine Not even milk for a cup of tea. But seriously, I spent . . .

Alan I'm sorry. We've got the bits left over from the journey.

Justine That'll be half a sandwich and a yogurt drink.

Alan And the bag of jelly sweets you confiscated.

Justine Give us them.

Alan takes the jelly sweets out of his pocket. Justine takes a couple out of the bag.

A cola bottle and a wibbly snake will have to suffice. So what do we do now? Go to bed? It's only five past nine.

Bronwyn appears at the canvas door. She whispers through the flap. She's got a slight Welsh accent. She's quite stressed but determined to keep it together.

Bronwyn Hello? *Noswaith dda.*

Justine Who now?

Bronwyn (*whispering*) Sorry to disturb you. *Croeso, croeso.* It's just Bronwyn, I run the place. Wanted to say hello. Is now not a good time?

Alan Come on in.

Bronwyn Hi, sorry I wasn't here earlier. Bronwyn.

Alan We've only just arrived.

Bronwyn Now don't tell me. I take great pride in remembering the name of everyone who's booked. Adam and Janet.

Alan Alan and Justine, near enough.

Bronwyn I should stop doing that. I always get it wrong. (*She continues to whisper.*) Me or my husband would normally be here to greet you but he's away for a couple of days. All a bit chaotic. Did you get the welcome pack?

Justine Yeah, yeah. You don't need to . . . They'll sleep through anything.

Alan We love what you've done here.

Justine Little home from home.

Bronwyn You're on top of the fire and lamp. And the bedding's all in order? Sheets, towels?

Alan It's all fine.

Justine We were slightly concerned about the mouse.

Bronwyn Sorry?

Alan Does it live behind here (*the coolbox*)? Or all through the tent?

Justine takes out the note and hands it to Bronwyn.

Justine Is it big? I know it's camping but I'm not really up for sharing the tent with wildlife.

Bronwyn This is meant to say 'house'. It's a little map of where everything is.

Alan Oh.

Bronwyn It is awful. No wonder I failed art. But that's the farmhouse, your tent . . .

Alan And the drawing of the mouse?

Bronwyn That's Elsie the pig. I'm so sorry. We're meant to get some proper maps printed but . . .

Alan We like it that it's all home-made and farmy.

Bronwyn You've got my number if you need anything.

Justine You might want to write that down again.

Bronwyn Oh, okay. (*She roots through her pockets for a pen.*) There's the little shop up at the farmhouse. It's a bit low on food, I'll do a shop in the morning. Just write down anything you buy and we tot it up at the end. The showers and compost loo are up there.

Alan Great.

Bronwyn There's fresh eggs each day. If you just go into the coop and help yourselves. I'll give the kids a tour of the farm tomorrow. Is that good for you? (*She's found a pen. She tries it.*) That doesn't work. (*She roots for another one.*)

Justine They'd love that.

Alan So you grew up here?

Bronwyn This was our family farm. Been passed down through the generations. Used to be a full working farm, that faded out and we're getting it back to where it was. Just the chickens and pig but we're getting more. I should be up at the farmhouse but if not I'll be down in the town. I'm not far if you call. Kids just love it on the field here and playing in the stream. There's some great walks. What else?

Justine This chair's a bit . . .

Bronwyn I'll get you a new one.

Justine goes into one of their bags and finds a pen.

Ta. (*She writes her phone number down.*) And were you the couple that wanted to cancel?

Justine Oh yeah . . .

Bronwyn I'm sorry I couldn't give you a refund. The payments all go through the Hedge Farms website which brings all the farms together. If it was up to me . . .

Justine It's fine.

Alan Just . . .

Justine Something out of our control.

Alan But we sorted it and we're glad we're here now.

Bronwyn That's good.

Alistair and Amanda appear from the left outside the tent. Amanda with a note in her hand.

Alistair She is in there. I can hear her.

Amanda Quick before she disappears again.

Amanda enters.

Sorry to disturb you. You can't see me. I'm not here. We just wanted to give this to Bronwyn.

Bronwyn Oh right. Is everything okay?

Amanda Yes, yes. Just a couple of little queries.

Alan You can come in.

Amanda No, we don't want to invade.

Alistair (*from outside tent*) We'll acquaint ourselves tomorrow.

Alan It's fine.

Amanda You sure?

Alan Of course.

Amanda holds open the flap for Alistair to enter.

Amanda Hi, I'm Amanda and this is Alistair.

Alistair Hey.

Alan Alan and Justine.

Justine Y'alright?

Amanda hands Bronwyn the note.

Amanda Don't look at it now. Just a few questions for you to get back to us on. We were going to drop it off at the farmhouse but we heard you in here.

Alistair You settling in?

Alan Just about.

Bronwyn opens the note behind them all and starts reading it.

Alistair We've been here since yesterday. You're going to love it. Been windsurfing down on the lake today.

Amanda That water's cold. Thank God we brought the wetsuits. But amazing.

Alistair You've got a great fire. If you have any problems in that department, give Bridget, next door, a shout. She sorted ours out.

Amanda And did all our dishes for some reason.

Bronwyn turns the page. There's two pages.

Bronwyn I can get you more bedding and towels.

Amanda Please don't look at it now. We'll talk about it later.

Bronwyn Some of this, is just how it is here. The solar shower is . . . solar. If there's not much sunshine it doesn't get very hot.

Amanda It was fine yesterday but it was cloudy today so . . . I just sort of flicked the water on me. Isn't there back-up? A booster?

Bronwyn That would sort of defeat the purpose. And there's nothing much I can do about the smell of the compost toilet either.

Amanda I've learnt to hold my breath but the children won't go anywhere near it.

Alan comfort-eats the jelly sweets.

Alistair (*to Justine*) You travelled far?

Justine No, no. Only took us a couple of hours.

Amanda Camilla had an idea. If you wanted to keep with the 'at-one-with-nature' vibe you could hang some bunches of lavender up. Might stop some of the initial retching when you walk in.

Bronwyn And I don't know what I can do about more animals on the farm, this week.

Amanda We understood it was a working farm. (*To Justine and Alan.*) There's hardly any animals. (*To Bronwyn.*) How much do a couple of sheep cost?

Bronwyn We're only a small farm. We are going to get more livestock. I'd love to get some sheep, do my own wool and knitting.

Justine (*keeping the peace*) That'd be nice.

Bronwyn Did you get eggs from the coop this morning?

Alistair Yes, lovely. I made a gorgeous frittata.

Bronwyn I'll get you some more board games.

Amanda Only if you can, we don't want you to go to any trouble.

Bronwyn (*reading*) 'And a garlic press and parmesan grater . . .' You know we've only just started doing the camping on the farm this year. You're our third lot of couples. It's still early days here. Big learning curve.

Amanda I know, but should we lose out because we're the first ones?

Alistair You just see what you can do.

Amanda Let us know which ones you can action and then we can talk about any which are still problematic. Moving forward we just want to get the best out of this holiday.

Bronwyn starts crying.

Alistair Oh dear.

Amanda Right.

Justine Don't get upset.

Bronwyn I'm sorry, it's been a long day.

Amanda You go and get an early night and we'll talk another time.

Bronwyn I'm trying my best.

Alistair Of course you are.

Amanda Let's talk when you're feeling less emotional.

Bronwyn It's been one of those days, weeks. I can't believe I . . . So not like me. How embarrassing.

Alan Don't worry.

Bronwyn I'm going to go before I make more of a fool of myself . . . Night, everyone. So sorry.

Justine Night, see ya.

Alan Night.

Bronwyn leaves the tent. She heads out dazed to the left then realises it's the wrong way and turns right to go home to the farmhouse.

Justine Poor thing.

Amanda I did tell her she wasn't meant to read it now.

Alistair And the children drew on a smiling chicken and love-hearts and kisses.

Alan I don't think it was the presentation that was the problem.

Justine Who knows what she's going through?

Amanda I don't know whether I buy it.

Justine Sorry?

Amanda The crying. Wasn't it slightly passive-aggressive?

Alan I think she just got upset.

Amanda If I start crying, especially if I'm in the wrong, it just shuts down everything. You can't discuss the problem and then you end up having to comfort them.

Justine I don't think it was like that.

Amanda I wasn't being horrible, was I?

Alistair No, that was nowhere near you being horrible.

Amanda It just makes me feel bad for asking a few questions. Women are the worst culprits.

Justine She seemed genuinely upset.

Amanda Well, does she need to be doing that here? She's running a business, if she's not up to it . . .

Alistair I know it hasn't lived up to your expectations. (*Mock under his breath.*) I think it's wonderful.

Amanda (*to Alan*) Are you happy with the way it is here?

Alan We've literally only just arrived. But we like it . . .

Amanda She's providing a service and in this day and age you can't do things by halves. And for the money it costs.

Justine I hate complaining.

Alan We're terrible.

Alistair Amanda loves it.

Justine She said she'd take the kids on a tour of the farm tomorrow.

Amanda Wait until you see it, I don't know if you could really call it a farm. Point 7b on our list.

Alistair The children love it. We've hardly left the site.

Amanda Not that we've been camping before. Friends have done this and said how wonderful it is.

Alistair We must have you round for dinner one night. Put the children to bed. We've got tons of drink. Play some games. All get to know each other. That's what these holidays are all about.

Alan We'd love that.

Amanda We'll see you tomorrow no doubt.

Alistair We were having an early night, but then Amanda heard Blodwyn.

He pinches Amanda's bottom.

Come on then, you.

Amanda and Alistair leave and head back to their tent.

Justine Give us those jelly sweets. I need them.

Alan There's none left. I comfort-ate them while they were here.

Justine We don't have to hang out with them, you know.

Alan We can though.

Justine God, I need something to eat. I'd love a cup of tea. No milk.

Alan One of them will have some. I'll go . . .

Alan goes out and heads to the right-hand side.
Justine's feeling cold. She goes to the bags and looks for some warm clothes. She finds a hooded top of Alan's and puts it on with the hood up. Pulling the string tight round her face. She adds more logs to the fire.

Justine Pyramid. Pyramid.

She fills the kettle with water and puts it on the stove. She tidies round the place to make it look more homely. Moving bags out of the way and lighting tea lights. She stands back to admire her efforts. She's pleased with her work.
Alan comes back from the right with a two-pinter of milk, two tea bags and four biscuits wrapped in cling film.

Alan Check this out. Milk, tea bags and chocolate Hobnobs. A triumph. I feel like I've just gone out and slain a wildebeest for tea.

Justine Kettle's on.

Alan I'm liking what you've done with the place.

Justine I could really get into this.

Alan You're looking . . . lovely.

Justine takes her hood down.

You should see the food they've got. It's like Waitrose. There were various biscuits hidden in the 'special cupboard' out of reach of the kids. She took four out and wrapped them in cling.

Justine (*sarcastic*) That's so generous. Just check on the kids.

She goes through to the bedrooms.
  Alan puts a tea bag in each mug. He grabs a chair to move it in front of the stove but as he does a leg falls off. In a moment of frustration, he bangs the chair against the floor a few times, making a loud noise.

Thomas (*off*) Mum . . .

Justine (*off*) Shush, shush. Go back to sleep.

Alan stops and takes a deep breath. He calmly moves the broken chair and places it at the table out of sight. He takes another chair. Gives it a shake to see if it's solid and places it in front of the stove and sits on it.
  Justine comes back out.

What was that noise?

Alan Doesn't matter.

Justine What was it? It woke Thomas up. He's gone back to sleep now.

Alan It was just the chair.

Justine And what?

Alan The broken chair. I was moving it and I knocked it. Okay?

Justine I was only asking.

Alan I was only saying.

Justine Just very loud in the middle of all this quiet.

Alan Will you stop going on about it?

Justine Okay. I won't say another word.

Alan (*under his breath*) For fuck's sake.

Justine What are you getting all –?

Alan Just leave it, leave it.

*Justine gets a chair and brings it near to the burner,
next to Alan. A tense atmosphere hangs in the air.*
   *They both get warm. A warm orange glow fills the
room. They both sit watching the kettle.*

Justine I wish there was something more comfortable to
sit on than these rickety old chairs.

   Pause.

Is it even getting hot?

   Alan touches the kettle with his finger.

Alan Not even warm.

   *They sit and watch. Justine looks at her watch. Alan
looks to her for the time.*

Justine Nine fifteen.

   *Alan passes Justine a chocolate Hobnob. They both
eat one each as they watch the kettle – not boiling.*

   Blackout.

SCENE TWO

*Next morning. Outside the tent. The flaps half pinned
back to create an entrance. A grey sky. Alan is sitting on
a deckchair with his book. He's wrapped up warm. He
tries to read but can't get interested.*
   *Justine enters from the right with a soap bag, a towel
over her arm and an opened box of muesli bars.*

Justine (*to kids off*) Of course you can play in that tree,
but do you want to put something warmer on?
   I don't believe you're too hot, it's practically minus
whatever.
   If you don't put something warmer on we're going
home. Fairy glen or no fairy glen.

Bridget and Rory have come out of their tent. Across to the right. We can't see them. Justine becomes aware of them.

(*To Bridget and Rory.*) Morning. (*To Alan.*) This is just what I wanted, shouting at my kids in a field in front of complete strangers. (*Quiet.*) Is he on the cider already? Look, he's pouring it into a mug so it looks like tea.

Justine goes into the tent. Alan surreptitiously looks over.

Alan (*shouting over*) Hi. Morning. I think we could be in for a good one today. There's a little speck of blue coming through.

Justine comes out of the tent with two hooded sweatshirts for the kids.

If they're too cold they'll tell us.

Justine All she's got on is her favourite summer dress. She'll catch her death.

Alan Look, next door's kids have joined them. All playing together.

Justine marches off to the right.

Justine Come on, down from that tree while I put this on you.
Look, these other children have got warm clothes on.
You either get down from that tree or I'll climb up after you.

Alan (*looking over to the other couple*) They've both only just got over colds.

Justine comes back minus sweatshirts.

Justine That's better.

31

Justine stands watching the kids play. Alan breathes in deeply.

Alan Oh, this is the life. Smell that fresh air.

Justine I can smell something else. Farm life.

Alan Bits of blue there. That cloud there is going to shift and then we're going to be in for a scorcher.

Justine Where's the blue?

Alan Just there in the distance, if you squint. I could live somewhere like this. Wouldn't it be nice to have our own little farm? Or run a country post office?

Justine No eggs. The others must have been up early and got them all. Didn't even see any hens.

Alan They're free range, they'll be wandering about.

Justine But we saw the pig. They liked that.

Alan I've got the burner on.

Justine Did you (*making the shape*) pyramid?

Alan I did, it's the secret. I reckon it takes a good half hour to warm up and I've measured out the exact amount of water for two cups. We've still got the two bags we didn't use from last night.

Justine So is this all aimed at people who've got everything? There's nothing left to have, so we pretend we haven't got the things we can't live without. We've got machines which make toast in thirty seconds. So let's go to a field and make toast at two hours per slice. Flushing toilets, light, heat. Let's just make everything take twenty times longer and much more difficult. These are even like pretend houses with windows, doors, bedrooms and kitchens. Is it like we're children again and this is one big wendy house?

Alan Didn't you sleep?

Justine No real food in the shop. (*Handing him a muesli bar.*) A muesli bar. That's breakfast. There was a pack of them. They've had two each.

Alan Right.

Alan eats the muesli bar. Justine stands watching the children.

Justine What shall we do today? Let's go out. There's that castle somewhere near. It's free, I think.

Alan Come and sit down. Let's just rest, relax, be on holiday.

Justine (*she looks over to Alistair and Amanda's tent*) No sign of the Camerons this morning? Their kids have been sitting outside that tent doing a jigsaw each in silence for hours. Mia said, 'Do you want to come and play with us?' They just looked at her like she was an alien. I asked them if they were warm enough. The older one said, 'There's no such thing as bad weather, just inappropriate clothing.' I said, 'Why don't you go and have a play with the others?' But she said, 'We're very content with our parallel play.'

Alan What the hell's that?

Justine No idea. Shall we go soon?

Alan I'm trying to read this.

Alan looks back to his book. Justine looks out.
Bridget and Rory come over. Rory drinks from a mug with cider in it.

Bridget Morning.

Rory Morning.

Bridget We just had a lovely omelette. Fresh eggs. The children were up at six, ran up and got the eggs.

Rory It's great, you just go into their coop and there they are just sitting in the little mounds of straw. The eggs. The hens are very elusive.

Justine Hopefully we'll get some tomorrow. Or from the supermarket.

Rory They do taste different. Much fresher. Lovely golden yolks.

Bridget We always buy free-range and organic anyway. Don't you?

Alan Yeah, yeah.

Justine I don't know if there's much difference, well, in taste.

Bridget It's not all about that, is it? You want to know the welfare of the animals is good.

Justine Yeah.

They look out at the kids.

Rory Isn't it great they're all playing together?

Alan Oh yeah.

Bridget It's so important, play, isn't it?

Justine I suppose so.

Bridget You know, just simple play. No TV or computer games or over-stimulation, just their own imaginations. We have no electronic devices during the week. It's a treat at weekends.

Justine Poor kids.

Bridget That's what's great about here. Back to basics. No electricity, so no TV, internet . . . (*Shouting across to the children,*) Now play nicely, Harry. What have I told you before about kicking? That's it, all together, nicely.

34

You go behind Mia, Harry. One at a time. Now it's your turn. That's it.

Rory I learnt most of the stuff I know from watching telly.

Alan Me too.

Bridget (*to the children*) I know a great game you can play.

Rory I think they're quite happy with the game they're playing.

Bridget (*to the children*) Look at these wonderful clouds. When it's your turn, why don't you see if you can name a cloud? Look, that's a cumulus and a nimbostratus. I've taught them the names of clouds.

Justine They'll have a field day here. Oh look at this one over here, big blackus rainus cloudus.

Bridget (*to the children*) There isn't one called that.

Justine So what age do you teach?

Bridget How did you know I was a teacher?

Justine A wild guess.

Bridget We're not both teachers. Rory's a . . . a . . . oh, what is it?

Rory She still doesn't know what I do. All she knows is I work in an office and I hate it.

Justine Oh, one of *those* jobs.

Bridget How could you tell I was a teacher? Well, actually I can always tell when I meet one. There's a certain engagement, enthusiasm for ideas, wanting to know more.

Justine (*half sarcastic*) Yeah. that's it.

Bridget I work in primary, with the year fours. They're just at that age where they're still pliable and nice but you can do interesting stuff with them. Egypt, Henry the Eighth, the Fire of London.

Alan What's 'parallel play'

Bridget It's where you have children doing different activities at the same time. At a table together. Why?

Alan Just curious.

Rory What do you do?

Justine looks to Alan.

Alan I . . . We've got our own business.

Rory Yeah?

Alan Yeah, yeah. Landscaping. Playgrounds, sports pitches in schools. We deal with teachers a lot. (*To Justine.*) That's probably how you could tell.

Justine Hmm, yeah.

Rory What a great business.

Alan I do all the designing and labouring, Justine runs the office.

Rory How's it going, in the present climate?

Alan We're holding on. Lost a few contracts, but we're keeping our head above water. (*He looks into the tent.*) Kettle's boiling. At last.

He goes inside.

Rory I'd love to be my own boss. I hate my job, working for someone else. My boss is a see-you-next-Tuesday.

Bridget Rory.

Rory (*to children*) Harry. What have I told you about punching your sister in the face? (*Heading off to deal* *with the children.*) Now, what do you say to your sister? (*Off.*) Now like you mean it.

Bridget Oh, have you got that money?

Justine Sorry?

Bridget For the milk, biscuits and tea bags?

Justine's speechless.

From last night.

Justine Of course, how much do we owe you?

Bridget It was a two-pinter, two tea bags and . . . the biscuits.

Justine Four biscuits.

Bridget Let's call it one pound twenty.

Justine I haven't got any on me just now . . . Alan, you got any change, love?

Alan (*from inside*) What for?

Justine For the stuff we borrowed off them last night.

Bridget 'From'.

Justine Sorry?

Bridget It's, 'for the stuff we borrowed *from* them last night'.

Rory (*off*) You're not correcting people's grammar again are you, Bridget?

Bridget You don't mind, do you?

Justine The money or the grammar? No, it's all fine. One pound twenty she, Bridget, wants. (*To Bridget.*) Have I said that right? (*To Alan.*) For the milk, two tea bags and four chocolate Hobnobs.

Alan (*coming out*) I've got one fifty.

Bridget I haven't got any . . . Let me see if Rory's got change.

Alan It doesn't matter. Have the one fifty.

Bridget No, I couldn't.

Justine Just take it.

Bridget I'd say let's make it a pound but the milk cost nearly a pound on its own.

Justine And we wouldn't want you to be out of pocket.

Bridget Okay. (*She takes the money.*) If you want anything else just let us know.

Alan Sure.

Bridget heads back to her tent.

Justine I'm stunned.

Alan Shush.

Justine I feel like saying, 'We haven't used the tea bags yet, you can have them back.' 'Are Hobnobs more than digestives? Without chocolate, would that be less?'

Alan It's done now.

Justine 'If we want anything else'? Oh yeah, she thinks she's got a right little racket going on.

Alan Maybe they're really struggling with money.

Alan heads inside.   .

Justine D'you think? Like we're loaded.

Alan (*from inside tent*) They said times had been tough.

Justine I know, but . . . What are we doing here?

Alan comes out with two mugs of tea.

Alan Tea's ready. There we go.

Justine Great. What a treat.

Alan I know.

They both drink. Pause.

Justine That's the worst cup of tea I've ever tasted.

Alan Undrinkable. All part of the experience. Back to my book now.

Justine Aren't we going out? How many years have you been reading that book for?

Alan Everyone says it's really good. This is my third go. But when I pick it back up I don't know whether to start again from the beginning or from the point where I last was.

Justine You're not some lesser person if you don't read books all the time. Come on . . .

Alan (*jumping up*) Let's go out. Go to this castle. I'll get ready.

He goes back inside.

Justine Okay, great. I'm going to go mad if I stay here all day. I'll get the kids.

Rory comes back over from the children, drinking from his mug. He stands awkwardly next to Justine.

Rory I love those children. Even when they're a pain.

Justine isn't sure what to say.

Rory I'm so happy but yet so sad. Being here.

Justine Right.

Rory We just get on so well when we're all together. It makes me sad that I know it's not going to last.

Justine That's what holidays are like, aren't they? You don't want to go back to what you've left behind. God, I understand that.

Rory I just wish we could stay here for ever.

Justine You like it that much?

Rory Maybe she'll see that we're better together than we are apart.

Justine (*not understanding*) Yeah.

Rory I know the children love it and with us, it's just like old times. We have our moments but even her bossing me about or our little tiffs I enjoy. I'm just dreading the day we leave and they all go to the house and I go back to my hovel.

Justine You don't all live together?

Rory Oh no, did you think we did?

Justine Well, yeah.

Rory We're not a couple, me and Bridget.

Justine Oh, right.

Rory We were. Married and everything, but we split up a few years ago. Well, Bridget ended it.

Justine But you still come on holiday together?

Rory Never before, not since she dumped me.

Justine It's good you get on so well that you want to go away together. That's pretty rare.

Rory We don't back home. Most of the time it's hell. It's all on her terms. She's in control of when I see my children. She withholds them if she's in a bad mood or if I put the slightest foot wrong. She'll call and says there's a change of plan and there's nothing I can do about it. 'Oh yeah, we're going to my mother's in Edinburgh for the weekend now. You'll just have to see them in a fortnight's time.' She's vile to me but I still love her.

Justine Right.

Rory We couldn't afford two separate holidays. It was her idea and I jumped at the chance to be a family again. I hate camping. Hated it since those awful holidays as a child. We're in the bunk beds. The children have got the double bed.

Justine Oh, right.

Rory I thought we were happy, then one day she said she'd had enough. She'd gone off me. It was over and I had to move out. She'd have the children full time. They could come and stay with me occasionally and I'd get visitation rights. I fought to keep them but the mum always wins. So that was that. I moved out of our lovely family home. To a bedsit miles away. I can't even afford to live near them. It's like I'm a student again. Like my whole life with children never happened. I haven't even got a spare room. When the children come to stay they sleep in my bed and I go on the sofa. I just work, come home and watch telly and drink on my own. I had a life and now I've got nothing. It's awful.

He starts crying.

Justine Oh, don't cry.

Alan comes out, changed.

Alan (*quiet*) D'you know where . . .? (*He sees Rory crying.*) Oh.

He goes back inside the tent.

Rory Look at me, I'm a joke. No wonder she doesn't want to be with me. I wasn't like this before. Children define you. When you've got them, everything's about them and sometimes it's crazy, but it's a full and rich life. Now it's like I'm a pretend dad. When I do have them I feel I have to do activities with them. Go to the cinema, the park, but what I loved before was just having them around. Watching telly together, them playing in their rooms, getting on with their lives. The day-to-day stuff. Life. It's all gone now. I'm so sorry.

Justine Don't worry.

Rory They bond you, children, don't they. I feel stronger when I'm with them. You can use them to hide behind. You don't have to reveal anything of yourself to anyone, you can just talk about your kids and it seems you're being open and honest. Or you can literally sit them on your lap and use them as a defence shield, so nobody can get to you. I'm just . . . I didn't think we'd have such a good time here . . . I'm just so happy, really . . .

He strolls back over to his tent. Alan comes out.

Alan What's going on there?

Justine Shush. Tell you in a bit.

Alan I'm ready.

Justine Okay.

Alistair strolls over dressed in the latest running gear. He limbers up in front of them.

Alistair Morning.

Alan Morning.

Justine Hi. I'll get the kids.

Justine goes off to the kids.

Alistair How was your first night? Sleep well?

Alan Actually, yeah. Quite cosy once we bedded down, got the bedsocks on and twenty layers. We did have a round of musical beds in the night but that's to be expected.

Alistair Like musical chairs? You played that in the middle of the night?

Alan You know, one gets in with you, then another and there's no room. So you end up getting out and into one of their beds. Then they move back. You never end up in the bed you started in.

Alistair We don't have any of that. The children know they can't get into bed with us.

Alan But sometimes they must wake up or have nightmares.

Alistair They just go back to sleep. If they know they can't get in with us, it's not an option, then there's no problem.

Alan Right.

Alistair But what happens if you want some time to yourself. Time for you? You know . . .

Alan Well . . .

Alistair It must affect your sex life?

Alan Well . . .

Alistair When do you and your wife get time to . . .?

Alan We find time. Although, I don't know a night since we've had them where they haven't got into bed with us.

Alistair This morning they knew we were having a lie-in. So they just get up and do their own thing. They knew we were having mum-and-dad time.

Alan Okay, right, yeah.

Alistair This is our holiday. It's not just about the children.

Justine comes back.

Justine Oh hi. (*To Alan.*) They've found some creature that they want to show you. They're very excited. They won't move until you've seen it. I'll get ready.

Alan goes off to the kids.

Alistair So, you should definitely come round for dinner one night. We've got some great beer and wine. Amanda's a brilliant cook. Put the children to bed. Drink and be merry.

Justine Yeah, yeah.

Alistair They can be tricky, these holidays where you're thrown in with other people. Could be a nightmare. But I think we're all going to get on well.

Justine And the kids seem to be having a great time together.

They both look over.

Alistair Ours can be a bit drippy sometimes. Look at them. (*Shouting across to their tent.*) Go on, play with the others. They don't bite. (*He looks out.*) Look at this view. Isn't it great to get away? To leave all your worries behind and just stop and relax.

Justine I'm not quite there yet. My head's still half at home.

Alistair By the end of the day you'll be settled. Took me a while . . . I'm not a nature person. More of a towny.

Justine Me too. Makes me nervous, all this space and quiet.

Alistair And mud. (*He spots something in the sky.*) Look, look. Is that a falcon?

Justine No, it can't be.

Alistair It is. It is. A peregrine falcon.

Justine D'you get them round here?

Alistair Must do, yeah.

They both watch for a second in silence.

Justine What's it doing?

Alistair I think it's got something in it's sights. It's circling.

Justine Let me get Alan.

Justine moves to go. Alistair puts his hand out on her shoulder.

Alistair Wait, wait. It's going to go, going to dive.

Justine stops. They both watch as the bird swoops down. Alistair still with his hand on her shoulder. Which she's aware of.

Justine (*half to herself*) Wow.

Alistair takes away his hand.

I wonder what he was going after? A mouse or a rabbit?

Alistair Sheep?

Justine Small child?

Alistair Yeah, not interested in nature.

Justine Me neither. Hate it.

Alistair laughs. Justine drifts off in deep thought for a second. Pause. Alistair notices and watches her for a second. She snaps out of it.

Alistair Where did you go then?

Justine Sorry. Did I . . . ? I just . . .

Alistair You got something on your mind?

Justine No, no. Bit tired or – I don't know . . .

Alistair Everything okay?

Justine Yeah, yeah.

He looks at her, giving her the space to say more.

It's fine. I'm fine. Thanks.

A look, a moment between them.

Alistair Okay, I'll stop prying.

Alistair stretches some more.

Justine (*gabbling to fill the space*) I don't know how you could go for a run. That's the last thing I'd want to do.

Alistair I need to keep fit. Got the fat gene. If I don't keep on top of it, I balloon. And it's a chance to see the landscape. Do you work out?

Justine What d'you reckon? God, no. I went for a swim in March with the kids. But I never actually swim.

Alistair You don't do anything?

Justine This is all on stress and nervous energy. I did try Pilates recently but it was *so* boring.

Alistair (*he looks at her*) You've got a great arse.

Justine What?

Amanda comes over in her running gear.

Amanda Ready?

Justine and Alistair are awkward, like they've been caught.

Am I interrupting something?

Justine No. God, no. We're just . . . talking . . .

Amanda Right.

*The silence and awkwardness hangs longer.
Alan comes over.*

Alan What's going on here?

Justine We just saw a falcon.

Alan Where?

Alistair It's gone now.

Justine dashes into the tent.

Amanda (*to Alistair*) Ready? (*To Alan.*) You don't mind keeping an eye on our two do you? While we go for our run.

Alan I'm not sure what we're doing.

Alistair We won't be long. Hour, tops.

Alan I think we're just about to go into town.

Amanda You can do that later can't you? (*Looking out at the children.*) Ours are playing with all the other children now.

Alistair About bloody time. They'll be fine on their own anyway, they're quite resilient.

Amanda You can say no. If it's a problem.

Alan You know, actually . . .

Amanda Ah, thanks. See you in a while.

Amanda and Alistair jog off discussing the route.

Alistair (*off*) If we head down past the stream and then it should bring us round to the village.

Justine comes out with her jacket on, a bag over her shoulder, a leaflet in her hand and the children's coats.

Justine We can do the castle this morning, then the model village this afternoon. I've had a word with myself and I'm not going to moan any more. I'm going to enjoy this. (*Shouting across.*) Come on, kids, we're going on an adventure.

Alan There's no rush. Why don't we hang out here for a while?

Justine No, we're going out. If I stay here much longer I'm going to go crazy. Crazier. Do you want to shut this door, flap?

Alan But the kids are all having a great time now.

Justine (*seeing Alistair and Amanda disappearing*) Look at those two. Who's looking after their kids while they go off gallivanting?

Alan We are.

Justine No, we're going out.

Alan They just sort of railroaded me. They won't be long.

Justine Who do they think they are?

Alan We're just all mucking in. They did say they'd be fine on their own. We could just leave them to play.

Justine I couldn't live with myself if something happened to them.

They spot Rory coming towards them.

Alan What about . . . ask—

Rory She's just having a lie down. Got one of her heads. I know to stay out of her way. We'll be having a nice conversation and then I just get the look. The face. And I know she's got one of her heads. And she's just so horrible to me. The woman I love.

Alan Would you mind . . . ?

Rory It just makes me want to kill myself.

Alan Doesn't matter.

Rory Do you want anything from the shop?

Justine There's nothing up there. Just some mouldy bacon.

Rory Oh well, be nice to have a stroll. Out of her way. Can you keep an eye on the kids?

Justine Fine, of course. We're here, not doing anything. Take your time. Anything else we can do for you?

Rory No, no. Cheers, guys.

He strolls off.

Justine So what do we do now? Just wait? I can't believe . . . You knew we were going out.

Alan picks his book back up.

You just going to read, then? What am I meant to do? What the hell are we doing here?

He doesn't answer.

It's madness. This is the last thing we should be doing. And *what was* all that earlier? About what we do?

Alan What else could I say?

Justine The truth.

Alan We don't know these people. We're just here for one week with them. They don't need to know everything.

Justine You know what's going on at home now?

He looks back to his book.

It's all I can think about.

He doesn't answer.

Justine I know you're not really reading. Talk to me.

Alan I've said I don't want to talk about it. Not while we're here.

Justine Well, I want to talk about it.

Alan Find someone else to talk to, then.

Justine So you don't mind me telling any of these lot?

Alan I'd rather you didn't.

Justine Well, who then?

Alan Will you just get off my back?

She lets out a frustrated scream at the sky.

Justine Aaahhh! (*To the children, who've heard,*) No, I'm fine, kids. It's just Mum messing about. Making animal noises. Mooo. There's the cow. Baaa. There's the sheep. Nothing to worry about. (*To Alan.*) I'm getting back into bed.

She goes back inside the tent.

(*From inside.*) And if I could slam this flap I would.

Alan looks back to his book. He tries to read but it's not happening. He closes the book and looks out at the sky. Trying to keep a lid on it, determined not to explode.

Blackout.

End of Act One.

Act Two

A few days later. The inside of Bridget and Rory's tent. The same interior and layout as before with the same furniture, burner, etc. . . . Dressed differently. It's all very untidy with clothes, bikes and stuff everywhere. Though Bridget and Rory aren't concerned. There's half-eaten children's party food laid out on the table – though it's not really party food, it's all very healthy adult food. It's a sunny day outside. The wood-burner is lit and glowing warmly.

The tent is empty.

Bridget is leading games with the children loudly outside.

Bridget (*off*) Now all follow me. And if you drop it you've got to name another country and we're still on Europe remember . . . Okay, Mia dropped it. Everyone freeze. You've got to name a European country to stay in . . . You must know one . . . England? That is right but I'm afraid we've already had that. Three times in fact. So you're out! Everyone else keep going, but this time with a potato as well. Where are the potatoes, Rory?

Rory runs inside to get potatoes. He roots through the coolbox.

(*Off.*) Hold still, everyone. No moving. As solid as a statue, as quiet a church mouse. Shall we have a little song while we wait? (*She starts to sing.*) 'Oh dear, what can the matter be? Seven old ladies got locked in the lavatory. They were there from Sunday till Saturday. Nobody knew they were there.'

Rory runs back out with a handful of potatoes.

(*Off.*) He's back. Potato each. On we go. Walk, walk, walk . . .

Rory comes into the tent with Justine and Alan with mugs in their hands. Justine has a present with her.

Rory (*to Bridget*) I'm here if you need me.

Justine We'll just put his present here. It's nothing much.

Rory Very kind. I'm so glad you could come. We've hardly seen much of you these last few days.

Justine We've just been out and about. (*Warming herself.*) Oh, this fire's great.

Alan Justine's keen for us to make the most of our days and not sit round like we're on holiday.

Rory It's great to have a birthday to bring us all together.

Justine The kids didn't want to miss it.

Alan They love a party.

Rory opens a high-up cupboard full of drink and other goodies out of reach of the children.

Rory Who's for a top-up?

Alan I wouldn't say no. Same again.

Rory pours a beer into Alan's mug.

Justine How many's that been?

Alan Who's counting? Oh, it appears you are.

Justine No, just –

Alan (*quiet*) I'm on holiday. Can you lay off for a minute?

Bridget (*off*) And stop. Harry that time. The colour's changed, so now it's numbers. What's seven sevens?

Rory He knows this.

Bridget (*off*) Forty-nine. That's right. But you've dropped your potato. Another coat on. Rory. Another coat.

Rory grabs a jacket from the back of the chair and runs out.
Alan is deep in thought.

Justine If you're going to be in a sulk we shouldn't have come.

Alan To the party or on holiday?

Justine Both. I don't particularly want to be here either. But it's for the kids.

Alan You're not helping, always on my back.

Justine Well, if you're walking round with the grey clouds of doom over you the whole time . . .

Alan It's you going on about it.

Rory comes back in. He tops up Alan's drink and makes one for himself.

Bridget (*off*) And on.

Alan (*all smiles*) Cheers, mate. I'm liking this beer.

Rory It's organic.

Justine (*quiet, to Alan*) Glad you can turn it on for everyone else. (*To Rory.*) Why don't we use glasses? There should be some there. Or we could bring ours over.

Rory Bridget would prefer if we drank out of mugs. So it looks like tea. She doesn't want the children to know we're drinking-drinking. That's what we always do.

Alan moves to go back out.

Justine (*to Alan*) How about using brown paper bags like winos? I'd like the record to show that I am actually drinking tea.

Alan heads out.

Sod it. Go on, I will have a drink. Red wine please. I wouldn't normally drink at a kids' party.

Rory pours Justine a large mug of red wine.

Rory I've been drinking since eight this morning. It's great.

She takes a big sip of wine. Then another. They both look out of the flap.

Bridget (*off*) Five nines? Forty-five. Correct.

Rory I'm so proud of her. She's thought of everything.

Justine She certainly has that. I can't believe the laminated schedule.

Justine picks up a laminated schedule from the table.

Rory She's in her element. Packs a lot in.

Bridget (*off*) Eight sixes? Oh no, it's forty-eight. Another potato for you.

Justine Don't you feel this takes the fun out of it all? You can't just see what happens.

Rory You don't want any spontaneity or you'd never get anything done. She's always telling me.

Justine (*looking at the schedule*) What's next? We're still on 'educational team games' and then the treasure hunt. She's even put in toilet breaks.

Rory I'd give anything to have this all year round. Be a family again.

Alistair comes in with a box of drink.

Alistair Brought some more booze. It's like Oddbins in our tent.

Rory Brilliant. If you put it in the top cupboard out of reach of the little 'uns.

Alistair unpacks the contents – many wine and speciality beer bottles – into the high cupboard.

Bridget Oh no, Rafe's gone. You're out. Only two left in. Need another coat and hat, Rory.

Rory hurriedly grabs a coat and a hat and runs out.

(*Off.*) We've changed category, so while you're doing that see if you can name all of Henry the Eighth's wives . . .

Justine is at the table, looking for something to pick at.

Justine Look at this party food. If this was my birthday I'd be gutted. No wonder they've hardly touched it. Where's the sausage rolls, the sandwiches on cheap white bread, bowls of Monster Munch and Hula Hoops?

Alistair joins her.

Alistair No Jammie Dodgers.

Justine Or chocolate fingers.

Alistair Lentils? Mangetout?

Justine Even adults don't want to eat this crap.

Alistair You make all the fun stuff forbidden, it only makes it even more appealing.

Justine The way these are going, their kids will be on heroin by the time they're twelve.

Alistair (*laughing*) You're funny. Amanda's so intense.

Bridget (*off*) We've already had Pluto. We need another planet or you have to go back to the beginning. The moon, yes the moon will do. On you go. Whoever gets the red triangle could be the winner. Unless you drop everything and we start again.

Amanda comes in and heads over to top up her drink.

Amanda I can't take much more of that.

Alistair heads out, patting her bottom on the way.

Was it something I said?

Alistair No, I'm just . . .

Amanda He's not annoying you, is he?

Justine No, no, not at all.

Amanda Good. Let me know if I need to have a word. When we're away he thinks everyone has to get on, turns into this social secretary figure.

Justine Oh really.

Amanda picks at the food.

Amanda Are you and, what's he called . . . Alan, happy?

Justine Sorry?

Amanda It's quite straightforward. Are you happy, together?

Justine Oh well, I . . .

Amanda You look it. Like you both get on, like each other.

Justine Yeah, yeah. We have our ups and downs.

Amanda Do you still love him, still find him attractive?

Justine Oh God, I . . .

Amanda Have I touched a nerve?

Justine No, no. I'm just at a kids' birthday party in a tent in the middle of a field and this is not what I thought I'd be talking about . . .

Amanda I've gone too far, haven't I? Don't worry. Any sign of Bronwyn?

Justine Oh, er, no. I've called her for this tour of the farm but her phone's turned off the whole time.

Amanda Get used to it. She's useless. I saw her in one of the fields yesterday with a huge rifle.

Justine No?

Amanda Oh yeah. Looked mad as anything. Like she was hunting for something or someone.

Bridget (*off*) The winner is Thomas!

Amanda Just through sheer perseverance alone.

Justine Ah, did he win? (*At the flap.*) Well done. What do you win?

Bridget (*off, to Justine*) There's no prizes. I don't believe in them. It's the taking part that counts.

Justine (*coming back in*) All that palaver and there's no prize.

Bridget comes in. Rory joins her at the flap.

Bridget (*to Rory*) You keep them going while I get the treasure hunt ready. I went too fast on that last game and I'm all out of schedule.

Rory What shall I do?

Bridget Make something up. Keep them interested or we'll lose them.

Rory Like what?

Bridget I don't know. Just do it! I'm exhausted. Get them to do the alphabet backwards while running about.

Rory (*off*) Okay, kids, gather round . . .

Bridget God, it's hard work but I love it.

Justine I'm knackered just watching.

Bridget It's great for them. I find children learn so much more through kinaesthetic play. Especially boys.

Justine You know they don't have to be learning here. They are on holiday.

Bridget Children are always learning, sucking it all in. If it's not this it'll be something else. Look what I've got.

She looks around to see no children are about. She goes into another high cupboard and takes out a large bottle of Coca-Cola.

Do you want some?

Justine What's it got in it?

Bridget Coke. Coca-Cola. I don't let the children have it. But I have it as a treat now and again.

Justine Go blow your socks off. I thought it was absinthe the way you're acting.

Bridget Do you want some?

Justine Naah, I'll stick to red wine. Out of a mug.

Amanda Fine, thanks.

Bridget takes a big glug of Coke.

Bridget Right. Treasure hunt.

She puts on a pirate's hat, parrot on her shoulder and picks up her treasure-chest kit. Justine and Amanda share a look and try not to laugh. Bridget heads out.

Bronwyn enters.

Amanda Ah, the Scarlet Pimpernel.

Bronwyn You're going to be so pleased with me. I've done some of the things you asked.

New fresh towels, new board games. I've got a plan for the compost loo. And I'm working through everything else.

Justine Ah, that's great.

Amanda Here, I brought it with me in case we ever saw you again.

She takes out another written-out list.

Just a few other things we'd like looking at.

Amanda goes back outside. Bronwyn sits down with the list and reads it quietly. She puts her head in her hands.

Justine Drink?

Bronwyn nods. Justine hands Bronwyn a drink as she sits there staring into space.
Alistair, Rory and Alan come in – in the middle of a conversation. Rory tops up their drinks.

Alistair We've got it all worked out.

Alan Don't get carried away.

Rory It's times like these where we need to help others out.

Alistair Exactly. We're all in this together.

Bronwyn knocks back the drink and swiftly leaves.

Justine What are you boys scheming about?

Rory I was talking to Alan about your business and I think it'd be perfect for the school Bridge works at.

Alistair And Rafe and Camilla's school. Amanda's a governor. And I think once some of the other schools see what you've done they'll all want a piece. He's been showing us pictures on his phone and it looks amazing.

Rory (*to Justine*) Wouldn't it be great? And it'd get you work in other parts of the country. Go national.

Justine Yeah, yeah.

Alistair I know schools are your thing, but we need work doing on our patio. We could do it as a surprise for Amanda. She'd love it.

Rory You're going to be busy.

Rory passes Alan a topped-up drink.

Alan Cheers, mate.

Alan picks up a football.

Shall we have a kickabout in a bit?

Alistair Great idea.

Rory As long as it doesn't disrupt Bridget's schedule.

Alan We've already been told off once today.

Alistair I've got to be careful or I'll be back on the naughty step.

Alan laughs and throws the football to Alistair, who heads out with it in his hands. Rory follows. Alan chuckles to himself.

Justine What? Hello?

Alan Don't start.

Justine Me?

Alan This could get us back on our feet.

Justine There's no feet to get back on.

Alan It could be just what we need.

Justine Are you living in some alternative universe? It's over. We don't have a business any more.

Alan But maybe this will get the ball rolling again.

Justine We spent months trying to keep it going, doing everything we could, but it's over, you know that. We can't just start it all up again because two blokes in a field have said you can do their patios.

Alan Oh thanks, thanks a lot.

Justine I'm just stating the facts. It's much more complicated . . .

Alan drinks his drink and thinks. Pause.

I didn't mean . . .

Alan stares at the floor. He's looking very intense. She moves to reach out to him.

Oh, Alan . . .

Bridget comes back in, followed by Rory.

Bridget That's the treasure hunt all set up. I can rest for a moment while they're off jolly-rogering.

Alan goes out with his drink.

Rory (*to Bridget*) Is there anything else I can do?

Bridget Not for the minute. It's going really well, isn't it?

Rory Couldn't have gone better.

Bridget You were great today.

Justine tops up her drink.

Rory Do I get a gold star?

Bridget No, I mean it. I don't know what I would have done without you. How I would have got through all those games. Maybe it was a bit much combining snakes and ladders, Scrabble and simultaneous equations in that first game. But we make a great team.

She reaches out and puts her hand on his shoulder. He melts.
Justine looks out of the flap.

Rory Do you think?

Bridget I'm just so glad you're here. I'm sorry for earlier. For shouting.

Rory It's okay.

Bridget No, this is your holiday too.

Rory Want a drink?

Bridget I'm just on Coke. Oh go on then. In a mug.

Justine The first lot are back with their clues.

Bridget Already?

Rory quickly pours her a mug of red wine. She rushes out with it. Rory follows like a little puppy.

(*Off.*) Oh no, you're still missing two treasure chests. Back, back, off out you go.

Justine gets warm by the fire. Alistair enters and helps himself to another beer.

Alistair Alan was telling me you don't get much time to yourselves.

Justine What was he saying?

Alistair Just that the children are in and out of your beds at night. You don't get much quality time.

Justine He said that?

Alistair More or less.

Justine I've never heard him say that. Or anything like that. All I get is a grunt or two out of him.

Alistair It's not true?

Justine Well . . .

Alistair I know what it's like when you have kids, they take over. You've got to make time for each other. Or the spark goes and it doesn't come back.

Justine I think we should . . .

Alistair We all have our needs.

Justine Hmm.

Alistair You're a very attractive woman.

Justine Oh, okay, thanks, that's . . . I do feel particularly attractive at the moment. In this little number. You're really seeing me at my best. Shall we join the others?

Alistair Don't go yet. You don't want to go back out there.

Bridget (*off*) Yes, Holly's team's won. Who's going to be second?

Justine Maybe not.

Alistair Top-up?

Justine Oh, go on. Red wine numbs the pain.

Alistair Which pain?

Justine All pain.

Alistair I don't like to hear that.

Justine I'm joking. Half joking.

He tops up her mug and looks into her eyes. She looks at him as he does so. A brief beat, he reaches in quickly and kisses her on the lips passionately. She takes it, then breaks apart.

Oh God.

Alistair I'm sorry. I shouldn't have done that.

Justine I know, I know.

Alistair But I just wanted to . . .

Justine It's done now. We should go and . . .

Alistair Join the others, yeah . . .

Neither of them moves. Alistair moves towards her again. Justine looks towards the tent entrance.

Justine They're just there outside.

Alistair moves in and kisses her again. She kisses him back.

Now that's it. I don't do this.

Alistair But you are . . .

Alan (*off*) Justine?

She breaks apart quickly and moves away. She picks up her mug of wine, takes a glug and tries to look busy. Alan enters.

Still in here?

Justine Yeah, just keeping warm. This fire . . . is . . . great.

Alan Treasure hunt's done and these are all over-tired.

Justine (*not moving*) Right.

Alan You coming?

Justine Yeah, yeah.

64

Alistair I was just going to show you that thing . . .

Justine What was that?

Alistair You know. The book. The kids' book I was telling you about. Your two'll love it.

Justine Oh that . . .

Alan I can get them ready for bed. You can hang out here for a while.

Justine Yeah?

Alan I'll put the kettle on. If you come in an hour it should be boiled by then. You on the wine now?

Justine I've only had a couple . . .

Alan It was just, earlier on, you were telling me . . . I'll see you in a bit.

Justine Shouldn't be long.

Alan Mia said she wants a story from you but I'll start . . .

Justine I'm coming. I'll come now.

Alan Okay. (*To Alistair.*) See you later, mate.

Alistair Yeah, yeah, bye.

Alan goes.

Don't go.

Justine I have to, need to . . . I want to.

Alistair You sure? We're only just getting to know each other.

Justine No, no. This is not something I do.

Alistair We're here a few more days, till the weekend. Are you?

Justine Yes, but . . .

Alistair I want to see you on your own again.

Justine Shush. Oh God, oh God.

Alistair Come here.

He moves to kiss her.

Justine No.

Alistair Why not?

Justine Because.

He moves in again and kisses her. She lets him.

Amanda (*off*) Al? Alistair? Are you still in there?

Alistair Yes, coming . . .

He rushes out.
   Justine is left alone on stage. Deep in thought.

Blackout.

End of Act Two.

Interval.

Act Three

Outside the tent. Night.
The same set. This time it's Alistair and Amanda's tent.
Justine, Alan, Alistair, Amanda, Rory and Bridget are
all standing outside the tent in the darkness. Looking out
up at the sky. All in silence for a moment as we first see
them. They've just let off a Chinese lantern and are
watching as it goes higher into the sky. We can't see the
lantern. They all have drinks in their hands. Bridget has a
mug. Alan has a large box of cook's matches in his hands.

Alan Look at it go.

Amanda It's going straight towards that tree.

Justine No, no.

Rory Just missed it.

Amanda We could have burnt the whole farm down.

Justine Look how high it goes. We should have let the
kids see this.

Alistair It's good they're all in bed.

Alan And it only really works in the dark.

Justine There's something really magical about it. I wish
I could just float up up and away like that.

Pause. They all watch.

Bridget I don't know if I approve. They get wrapped
round animals' heads and strangle them to death.

Justine Is that true? They've been around for hundreds of
years in China.

Amanda Or what happens if one that's on fire lands on your house? While it's still on fire.

Bridget If it landed on your thatched roof . . .

Justine I imagine there's about eight thatched roofs in Britain.

Bridget Lifeguards hate them because they get mistaken for distress flares and are always sending out their lifeboats.

Justine I thought it was nice.

Alistair Me too.

Rory I can't see it now.

Alan There it is. No, that's a star. Lost it now. It's gone.

Justine searches the sky for it.

Justine There it is, right in the distance. Just see it. Twinkling.

Justine watches it in the distance, deep in thought.

Amanda Right, all inside. The starter's ready and the main won't take long.

Amanda, Bridget and Rory head inside. Justine doesn't move.

Alistair (*to Amanda*) Popping across to compost hell.

Alistair heads off to the right. Alan watches Justine for a second.

Alan (*to Justine*) You coming?

Justine Yeah, yeah.

Justine stays looking out at the sky. Deep in thought. He joins her.

Alan Come on, love.

Justine I can't believe it's our last night.

Alan I know.

Justine You feel you've got all the time in the world and then it's over.

Alan That's what holidays are like.

Justine It's gone. (*The Chinese lantern.*)

Alan You what?

Justine The . . . I don't want to go back.

Alan And I thought you didn't want to be here.

Justine What are we going back to?

Alan Shall we go and join the others?

Justine What do we do when we go back? Not just our business, but us. What *are* we going back to?

Alan (*moving to go*) I'm gonna –

Justine I don't know what you're thinking or feeling.

Alan Let's just have a good night, eh?

Justine I can't just switch off all these thoughts and feelings and worries. You might be able to bury your head in the sand but I can't.

Alan drinks his beer.

I'm scared.

Alan We'll talk about this tomorrow.

Justine Will we?

Alan I just want to have a good night. I'm going in. Coming?

Justine Let me check on the kids.

Alan You are gonna come back, aren't you?

He waits a second. She doesn't answer. Alan goes into the tent. Justine looks back out.

Bridget (*off*) Here he is.

Rory (*off*) You need another beer.

Justine moves to head over to her tent when Alistair appears behind her.

Justine (*half jumping*) Bloody hell. Where did you come from?

Alistair I was just –

Justine Lurking in the bushes.

Alistair Not quite. I've hardly seen you.

Justine We've been busy.

Alistair I thought you were avoiding me.

Justine What makes you think that?

Alistair I didn't think you'd come.

Justine Alan was very keen. The last night and all that. He felt we couldn't say no.

Alistair I'm glad you're here.

Justine I'd better go and check on the . . .

She moves to go.

Alistair You look lovely.

Justine It is dark.

Alistair Stay.

Justine I can't be . . .

Alistair I thought . . . The other day . . . it was fun.

Justine That's why I don't want it to go any further.

He comes up close to her.

Alistair But there's an attraction. Isn't there?

Justine I don't want to get into this. This is not me.

Alistair There's a part of you . . . that's excited.

Justine We leave tomorrow. Nothing can happen.

Alistair Let's just see. We can have some fun. You're so beautiful.

Justine Please stop it.

He reaches out to touch her and feels the back of her neck. She takes a deep breath and lets him continue.

Alistair It's alright. It's alright. You're so tense.

Justine Tell me about it.

He massages the back of her neck with his hand.

This is why I didn't want to come. Me and Alan are having such an awful time.

Alistair Shush.

She turns to look at him and kisses him passionately. A long passionate kiss. They break apart.

It's alright. It's okay.

Justine I don't know what I'm doing.

Alistair Don't think about it. Let's just have a nice night, few drinks. See what happens.

Justine Oh God . . .

Alistair (*a finger on her lips*) Shush. It's all going to be fine.

Justine But nothing can happen. How can it?

Alistair Don't think ahead, just . . .

He moves to kiss her again. The others all laugh and clap inside. Justine pulls away.

Bridget (*off*) Bravo. Bravo.

Justine The kids. Let me check on them.

She heads over to her tent.

Alistair See you back inside.

Alistair turns and heads into the tent. We follow him inside.

Inside the tent. The wood-burner is raging with various pots, pans and an authentic Moroccan tagine bubbling away. Many candles are lit round the place, hanging in lamps and a gas lamp is hanging over the table. The table is laid out for dinner with amazing dips and starters – all home-made by Amanda. It all looks quite magical and as if it was in an advert. Amanda is busy in her apron at the work surface, chopping and mixing ingredients. Alan, Rory and Bridget are sitting at the table eating the food and drinking. There are many real ales and ciders on the table. Rory and Alan are drinking them and comparing, as Alistair enters.

Amanda Where've you been?

Alistair Do you really want to know the ins and outs of my ablutions?

Amanda You've been for ever.

Bridget You're missing all this amazing, amazing food.

Rory And drink. Loving these beers.

Alan This is my favourite so far.

Alistair That one goes back centuries.

Rory It was made by blind monks.

72

Amanda That accounts for the toenail floating in it.

Alan Where did you get all these from?

Alistair I got my assistant to find them. I said I want the best traditional beers and ciders for camping. Apparently there's a specific website just for that. We've got half a brewery to get through before we go.

Amanda (*to Bridget*) It's so sweet, isn't it? The men and their beers.

Bridget What can we talk about? What do we have in common?

An awkward pause as Amanda thinks.

I'm sure we'll come up with something.

Amanda Oh yeah.

Alan Any sign of Justine out there?

Alistair Oh no.

Amanda I thought I could hear you talking to each other.

Alistair No, no. Not us. Is there anything I can do?

Alistair comes up behind Amanda, puts his arms round her and kisses her neck. She's busy checking instructions in a cook book.

Amanda What are you doing?

Alistair Just being affectionate.

Amanda Well, don't. Not while I'm cooking. Just sit down and keep out of my way.

Rory I wouldn't complain. We all need a little love.

Bridget I can't believe you brought cook books and everything with you. I'm a terrible cook.

Rory But you do try.

Amanda I love cooking. Following a recipe, creating order.

Alistair Some people would call it control.

Justine enters.

Alan There you are. All well?

Justine Yeah, fine. They're both fasto.

Alan You've got to try some of this before it all goes. I think this one's broad beans. Can you believe me eating broad beans?

Justine (*quiet*) You know, I'm feeling a bit off. Can we go?

Alan We haven't eaten yet. Can't just leave.

Justine Shush.

Alan What is it?

Justine I don't know. Something doesn't feel right.

Bridget What's this? You can't go, it's the last supper.

Rory We've hardly seen you the whole time we've been here.

Alistair And Amanda's gone to so much trouble.

Amanda I don't mind if you're not up to it. If you want to go and rest that's fine by me.

Alan Sip some water. Have some of this food, might sort you out.

Alistair Another glass of wine might do the trick.

Justine I don't want to make a big deal. Maybe I'll have some food and then call it a night.

Bridget (*with a full mouth*) Oh, this is . . . (*To Rory.*) Taste this.

She holds it out for him to have a bite. He's thrilled at the idea of sharing food. He takes a bite.

74

Rory Hmm, oh yes.

Bridget You didn't get any of the artichoke . . .

She holds it back at his mouth, so he can bite the artichoke.

Rory Hmm. Delicious.

Bridget finishes off the last of the piece.

Amanda (*half to herself*) Is that the last of the garlic? Do either of you have any?

Justine If you want family packs of Wotsits we're your man, otherwise . . .

Bridget I think we've got some. Have we?

Rory I'm not sure. Did we use it up in that spag bol?

Bridget No, I bought some more. I think.

Rory Yeah, we have, we have. I think it's in that basket with the onions.

Bridget Two secs.

Rory I can go for you.

Bridget It's fine.

Rory You sure?

Bridget Yeah, yeah.

Bridget heads out to her tent.

Alan So who's . . .

Rory starts to cry quietly.

Amanda Oh.

Justine You okay?

Rory Yes, yes. I'm just so happy.

Alistair You don't look it.

Rory I am. I'm just so emotional. It's moments like that, with the garlic, that do it for me.

Amanda Did I miss something?

Rory In those moments. Those exchanges we're a little unit. We're together in it. And I think of what could lie ahead. That we'll get back together. We've never got on so well. I can't quite believe it. And the children love it and they're saying they like Mummy and Daddy when we're here. That there's no fighting or name-calling. You hear of divorced couples getting back together. Seeing what they've missed. I don't want to jinx it, but when we get back I'm going to see what she says. Suggest we give it another go. Me move back in, renew our vows. Maybe I'm getting carried away.

Alistair tops up people's drinks and opens new beers for Rory and Alan. Putting his hand on Justine's shoulder as he moves about.

Alistair Why wait until you get back? If you're so happy and she's happy here, make the most of it. Seize the moment. Tell her tonight.

Rory D'you think?

Amanda Especially before she goes back to the misery of real life back home. You'll have lost her then.

Alistair You've got to take risks in life. If you feel passionate about something, go for it before it's too late. (*To Justine.*) Don't you think?

Justine I'd weigh everything up. Make sure you're not getting carried away in the moment and doing something you'll regret.

Alistair You'll regret it if you don't.

76

Alan (*to Alistair, as he passes him another beer*) Are you trying to get me drunk?

Alistair Yes.

Rory I think you might be right. I'm going to say it before we go. Maybe tonight.

Alistair Go for it!

Rory Yes, yes . . .

Alistair pours some wine into Justine's glass.

Alistair Try this wine – you'll love it.

Justine tastes it.

Justine Hmm, yeah.

Alan You feeling better?

Justine I'm alright just now.

Alistair Told you a drink would sort you out.

Alistair tops up her glass.

Alan He's trying to get us all drunk.

Alistair It's true, I am. (*To Amanda.*) How much longer before our main?

Amanda Still got a way to go.

Alistair takes out a pack of cigars.

Alistair Look what I've got. Little treat. Lads?

Amanda You don't have cigars before dinner.

Alistair There's no rules tonight. We can do whatever we want.

Amanda You're not smoking them in here. They'll stink out the place. Out.

Alistair We'll go outside.

Alan and Rory move to go.

Justine You don't smoke.

Alan I fancy one, with the lads.

Justine I'd like to see this.

Alistair We'll leave you ladies alone.

Alistair, Rory and Alan head out of the tent and round the side so we can't see them. A slight awkward beat as Justine and Amanda are left alone. Justine pours herself a wine. Amanda takes a food-mixer out from behind the work surface and whizzes up some herbs in it.

Justine Where did that come from? And how is it working? There's no electricity.

Amanda We brought it with us. And the little generator too. There's just some things you can't go without. Hairdryers, somewhere to charge our iPads . . . I know it's camping but there's no need for it to be primitive. The microwave's been a lifesaver. We've got a flat-screen television in our bedroom.

Justine No?

Amanda No.

Justine Oh.

Alan coughs heavily outside the tent.

I don't even know why he's trying to smoke.

Amanda You're just his type.

Justine Sorry?

Amanda Alistair. You're exactly what he goes for.

Justine I don't understand.

78

Amanda He has a type. You know what that means?

Justine Yeah.

Amanda You're it.

Justine Aren't you his type?

Amanda Evidently not. Well, not exclusively. You must know I'm not, as he's been after you since he first saw you.

Justine Sorry?

Amanda Don't be embarrassed. I'm quite used to it. So how far has he got?

Justine is open-mouthed. Pause.

He's got it all planned out. He seems to think you're up for it. Are you?

Justine is speechless.

You know. There's no point pretending, it's so obvious. The way he's been behaving, you were a dead cert. I thought he'd done all the groundwork. Didn't he use any of his lines? 'We all have our needs . . .'

Justine doesn't know what to say. She gulps back wine. Pause.

Is your husband . . . Alan really up for it? I wouldn't have thought he'd be . . .

Justine You what?

Amanda And I imagine Alistair will want to get rid of the other two. He wouldn't want to end up with *her* and I'm sure . . . Alan wouldn't.

Justine I really don't know what you're talking about.

Amanda What bit of it don't you understand?

Justine Do you mean . . .?

Justine thinks – it suddenly hits her what it all means.

Justine Oh my God.

Amanda Oh yeah.

Justine I mean you see it in films, car keys in the bowl and all that, but you don't think it actually goes on.

Amanda Alistair thinks it keeps him sane. Which is nice. He thinks it's going on everywhere.

Justine is taking it all in.

Did you think there was something more going on? That he liked you? That it was just about you and him?

Justine No, no, no . . .

Amanda You did, didn't you. Do you like him?

Justine You know, I don't know what your plan is but I want nothing to do with it.

Amanda It's not my doing. I'm no part of this. I'm no Rosemary to his Fred West.

Justine Then what . . .?

Amanda chops and prepares food through this – stopping now and again.

Amanda This is his thing. His fantasy, his thrill. I go along with it to some extent because . . . it's a deal I've made. Not with him. In my head. It's my way of keeping him. But I hate it, I hate him for wanting someone else. No matter how much he says it's 'just a bit of fun', it kills me. I know he loves me. What does it matter if he has a drunken fumble with some other woman? It's all the thought and planning that goes into it. It takes over him. Dinner parties, holidays, he's on the lookout. He's only actually done it twice. Both times I ended up with someone who wasn't interested either and we just chatted while he . . . But even if it doesn't happen he tries to make it happen. He wants to go to swinging parties in the suburbs. It'd be easier if he just went off and had flings and I knew nothing about them. Maybe he does. But he wants me to be part of it. Wants to see me having sex with another man, even a woman . . . I can't believe this is where I've ended up. The idea disgusts me. And here's me working like a slave. Trying to make everything perfect, be the perfect wife, keep him happy. What am I doing?

Amanda stops still for a moment.
Bridget comes back with the garlic. She hands it to Amanda.

Bridget There we go. Couldn't find it anywhere. Eventually found it in Rory's washbag. Don't know how it got there.

Amanda stands with the garlic in her hand. Not doing anything with it.

There's nothing wrong with it. I washed the toothpaste off.

Amanda I don't know what I'm doing. I can't do it any more.

Bridget I get like that. You're in the middle of a recipe and you don't know how you're going to make it to the end. Where are we? (*She reads the recipe.*) 'Three cloves of garlic' . . .

Justine We'll give you a hand.

Amanda sits down with a glass of wine.

Bridget (*to Justine*) She's even got all her timings written down. (*She looks at her watch and what's chopped out in front of her.*) We're right on schedule. Just like me. If you laminated this it'd be perfect. Wipe clean.

Justine Just this dressing to do.

Amanda (*getting back up*) The tagine should be . . .

81

Alan, Alistair and Rory enter from outside and sit back down. Light rain can be heard against the canvas.

Alistair This is what I like to see. All our women cooking for us.

Amanda (*under her breath to Justine*) Shall I just stab him now?

Alan It's starting to spit.

Bridget I love the sound of rain against canvas. And you're all snuggled up under the covers.

Rory Especially if you're with someone you love.

Bridget Yeah. That's nice.

Alistair (*to Justine and other women*) How we doing?

Justine blanks him. Alistair comes over to Amanda.

Everything going to plan, eh?

Amanda turns with a hot pan and nearly catches him.

Careful, dear, you nearly burnt me.

Amanda And we wouldn't want that now, would we?

Alistair sits down with the men and tops up their drinks while the women continue to cook.
Bronwyn appears with a big box full of dandelion wine. She's looking rattled.

Bronwyn *Noswaith dda*, everyone. *Noswaith dda*. (*She plonks down the box of wine and heads back out.*) Be right back.

Alistair Who asked her?

Justine Is it okay? I mentioned it. I found her sobbing in the pigsty earlier.

Alistair I can forgive, but Amanda will be furious.

Amanda I don't care any more.

Alistair She hardly addressed any of the issues on any of the lists you gave her.

Amanda I think there's more important things to worry about.

Alistair If you're happy. I'm only thinking of you.

Justine Ha!

Amanda Oh, are you now?

Bronwyn comes back in with a box of toys in her hands.

Bronwyn I wanted to see you all and apologise for being so crap. Crap, crap, crap. I've brought home-made dandelion wine. Gets you absolutely battered. Makes your wee green and fizzy but it is tremendous.

Alistair Jesus Christ.

Bronwyn And I've brought toys for the children. They're made by local craftsmen. All on me. There's little Welsh dolls for the girls. (*She takes out some strange-looking Welsh wooden dolls.*) Aren't they lovely? (*She dances one across the table.*) 'Hello, my name's Myfanwy, what's yours?'(*The doll's head falls off.*) That's not very good.

Alistair And a lovely big sharp nail underneath.

Bronwyn That's just a faulty one. (*She throws it back in the box.*) And I've got traditional Welsh guns for the boys.

Alan Welsh guns?

Bronwyn Oh, yes. All perfectly safe. They just fire little sticky pellets. See.

She sets one up and aims it at the Welsh dresser with crockery on it. She fires it. It shoots practically a real bullet, smashing some crockery to smithereens.

That's slightly more powerful than I was expecting. But the kids'll love 'em.

She puts the toys away.

Let's crack open the dandelion wine. All home-made on the farm by me. Not from the shop. Maybe from the shop.

She pours out wine into glasses.

Bridget I'll have mine in a mug.

They taste the wine.

Wow.

Alan Hmm, I like it.

Alistair It's like prosecco.

Justine Just like pop.

Rory All the fizziness has gone up my nose.

Bronwyn It goes down so easily. You open a bottle. Before you know it you've drank two and half and you're crawling round the farm on your hands and knees talking to animals that aren't there.

Alan Have you already had some this evening?

Bronwyn Teeny tiny sip.

Amanda Food's ready.

Amanda serves up the tagine with various sides of vegetables and rice, laying it out in bowls for everyone to help themselves. It looks amazing. Bridget helps serve it up. Justine is deep in thought.

Bridget This looks and smells incredible.

Alistair It'll taste amazing too. I'm so proud of her.

He kisses her.

Alan Wow, what is it?

Amanda Some Moroccan lamb tagine thing with veggies and rice. Let's not stand on ceremony. Tuck in, everyone.

They all start dishing up.
    Alistair tops up people's drinks. Justine puts her hand over her glass.

Justine None for me.

Alistair Oh, go on.

Justine No, I've sobered up all of a sudden.

Alistair Why's that? (*He tries to top up her drink.*) Go on.

Justine Didn't you hear me? I said no!

Alan Justine?

Justine I'm sorry, sorry.

Amanda This couscous could be hotter. Just give it a quick . . .

She takes the plate of couscous away, opens the cupboard with the microwave in and slams it inside.

Bronwyn I sometimes forget how well equipped these tents are. Didn't remember there was a microwave in there.

Alistair gets up and joins Amanda at the microwave.

Alistair (*whispered*) What's going on?

Amanda Don't ask me.

Amanda just smiles. Alistair sits down and tops up his drink.
    They all tuck in, in silence. Pause. Rory looks round and takes it all in.

Rory This feels like such a special night. (*To Bridget.*) Don't you think?

Bridget I suppose so.

Rory It's our last night before we go back to the grind, back to normality.

Bridget Yes, of course.

Rory And we've had such an incredible time. We've got on like never before.

Bridget I would never have believed it.

Rory I want it to be different when we go back. I don't want to go back to how it was before.

Bridget Neither do I.

Rory Really?

Bridget Yes. I've thought about it a lot while we're here and it's made me see things anew. I don't mind saying this in front of everyone. We're amongst friends. We could hardly talk to each other before. I was so angry most of the time. Didn't want to tell you anything. But now . . . I feel I can say anything to you. So when we go back . . .

Justine Do you want to do this here and now?

Rory There's no time like the present. Go on. You go first. I think I know.

Bridget Do you? Oh, the children have said . . .?

Rory They might have said something, they're so excited.

Bridget Well, I know they get on with him but you never know . . .

Rory What did you say?

Bridget I can't believe I'm finally saying this – about Dominic, and him moving in. The children have told you about him?

86

Rory Yeah, yeah. I know about . . . Dominic.

Bridget And they all get on so well. We've been going out now for over a year and I've been too scared to tell you about him. But I feel it's time to take it forward, for him to move in. I wanted you to know and be happy about it. It was your house. I thought you might not like it, but you're okay?

Rory Yeah, yeah. I think it's great. So happy for you.

Bridget What was it you wanted to say? Was it to do with that?

Rory Yeah. You know, just that we get on so well and we should *move forward* with our lives and become great friends. You've got him and . . . I've been seeing someone.

Bridget Have you? Oh that's great. Who?

Rory She's called . . .

He subtly tries to look round the room for inspiration. Amanda passes a bowl of steaming broccoli across to Justine in front of him.

Bro . . . Brock.

Bridget Brock. What an unusual name?

Rory She's Canadian. A Canadian scientist. Yeah. Does very important work. We're so happy.

Bridget I'm so pleased you're happy too. I'd sometimes thought that you wanted us to get back together.

He forces a laugh. She laughs too.

Rory Ah, no. Us two, no. That'd be the day. God, no. No, no, no. Never thinking that.

A long awkward silence, as he's protested too much. Rory opens another beer and fills his empty glass.

When it's full the bell rings on the microwave and breaks the silence. Amanda takes out the couscous. Rory really knocks back his beer.

Amanda Couscous anyone?

Alistair (*to Alan*) Oh yes, your business.

Alan What about it?

Alistair I've got you some work.

Alan Right.

Alistair Real proper work. A booking. I've convinced Amanda to let you do some work on the school grounds during the summer holidays.

Amanda We've been meaning to get it done for ages. We did have some contractors lined up but their company went bust.

Justine Poor people.

Alistair Their loss is your gain. That's business. So I don't know how you're fixed but it'd be just a few weeks' work as soon as you can during the summer holidays. It's a private school, they've got tons of money.

Amanda Alistair.

Alistair It's true isn't it?

Amanda Yes, but . . .

Alan Let's not talk about work now.

Alistair But this might be the last chance we see you. What do you reckon? It'd be doing up a playground and building a new play area.

Alan Let me look at the diary and I'll give you a call when we get back home.

Alistair Well, are you busy the next few weeks or not?

Alan Well . . .

Justine Alan's too polite. I don't think it's going to happen.

Alistair No, why not?

Justine Because –

Alan Can't we just leave this for now?

Alistair I thought you'd be pleased . . .

Justine It's just not happening. I, we don't want to take you up on your offer. Thanks for the . . . interest but it's not for us.

Amanda It's all off, Alistair.

Alistair But why wouldn't you? Especially in the current climate. We all know work is hard to come by.

Amanda It's a no, Alistair. Sometimes you've got to learn when no means no.

Alistair But you were so keen the other day.

Alan (*with a spike of anger*) Can you just leave it?

Alistair Okay, okay. Your loss.

> *Alan starts to drink more heavily and go into himself.
> A muffled voice comes from the bedrooms at the
> back of the tent.*

Justine What was that?

Camilla Mummy.

Amanda Shush. It's Camilla.

Camilla Mummy? Daddy?

Justine Ahh . . .

Amanda Keep your voice down.

Alistair She'll go back to sleep in a second.

Amanda Always does.

Camilla I'm scared.

Justine Oh God.

Alistair She knows if she creates a big fuss then we'll go to her.

Justine But listen to her, she sounds upset.

Camilla starts crying.

Alistair If she carries on she's going to wake her brother.

Camilla I'm scared, Mummy.

Justine She's terrified.

Alan (*quiet*) Justine, stay out of it.

Alistair No, she's not. What's she got to be scared of round here? She's completely safe.

Justine Does she know that?

Alistair Of course she does. She knows she's never in any danger ever. We tell her that all the time.

Amanda Should I go to her?

Alistair No.

Amanda But maybe I should . . .

Alistair That's not like you. What's got into you?

Camilla stops crying.

See, she's gone back to sleep now.

Justine Cried herself to sleep.

Amanda It won't do her any harm. If anything it'll do her some good. Toughen her up. If she realises that when something's wrong no one's going to come running to her. Make her more resilient.

Bronwyn I'm really confused. (*To Bridget and Rory.*) You're a couple, but you've got other partners?

Justine coughs and nearly chokes on her food. Alan pats her back.

Alan Did it go down the wrong way?

Justine nods as Alan helps her with a glass of water.

Bridget We're separated but we came away together for the children.

Rory (*under his breath*) I wish I'd never come.

Alan starts to knock back the drink more.

Bronwyn My husband's *left* me.

Amanda He's not away for a couple of days?

Bronwyn No. That's just what I say. I doubt I'll ever see him again.

Bridget Oh.

Bronwyn He hated it here. Lasted three weeks. And it was his stupid idea. 'Let's move back to that quaint little village where you come from and run a campsite on a farm.'

Amanda This isn't your family farm?

Bronwyn Oh no, that's all part of the mythology they like us to play out. I grew up on a council estate down in the town. We're not really meant to talk about it, but Hedge Farms Camping can't gag me. They're all franchises not real homespun family farms.

Alistair Like McDonald's. A lot of them are franchises.

Bronwyn They come and build the tents and give you all the kit. All the 'home-made' signs. They advertise you through the website and take a cut of whatever you make.

Alistair Of course. it's all a business.

Bronwyn It's run by a bloke who made all his money through hedge funds. Hence the name.

Justine Ugh.

Bronwyn As soon as we got here, tents built, he started going loo-lah. Just us two, up in that massive farmhouse all the time. And he was lost without his high-speed broadband. When the first bookings appeared and he realised he had to make beds, well . . . One day he went down to the village to get some bread and never came back.

Bridget Maybe he's been in an accident and he's in intensive care somewhere. Or he's got amnesia and doesn't know who he is.

Bronwyn I didn't for a minute think he hadn't left me. I had such a wonderful life before. Look at me. I used to be successful, popular, interesting. Now I'm some mental woman living in a cottage with a load of strangers camping in my field.

She starts crying.

Alistair Now her too.

Bronwyn I hated it here. That's why I left. But now I'm stuck here with bookings all summer.

Justine It'll work out.

Bronwyn And the finances don't add up so I'm haemorrhaging money. I'm hardly here because I've got another job to make ends meet. I'm working in a colostomy-bag factory in Rhyl by day. I worked there as a teenager. All the same staff, just twenty years older. Some have got their kids working on the conveyer belt next to them.

Justine The farm will start making money.

Bridget You've got the pig, the chickens, get some more. Pay for itself.

Bronwyn The animals are all for show. The pig is dying. It's got cancer. We got it for nothing. It's one big grunting tumour. And the hens. Have you ever seen them?

Rory We always miss them because they're free-range. They're off running about.

Bronwyn There's no hens. They were all eaten by foxes in the first week and they're too expensive to replace. I buy a load of the cheapest crappiest eggs from the market. They're not even free-range. And put them out before I go to bed. I throw on some muck and feathers to make them look authentic. It's all a sham. I hate it here. Hate the whole idea. Pretend-camping for people with more money than sense, no offence. And if anyone calls it glamping, I'll lamp them.

Justine starts crying.

Justine It's so sad.

Alistair What's she getting all upset about?

Justine When you try so hard. Try and do something different.

Alan Don't cry.

Rory Shall we talk about something else?

Alan Yeah.

Justine I can see she's a good person. She's trying.

Justine gives her a hug.

I know how you feel.

Alistair Is there something in that dandelion wine? It's all got very serious. We're meant to be on holiday. Let's have some fun. Who wants to play a game? A drinking game?

Amanda What about spin-the-bottle?

Alistair Yeah, yeah. (*He realises she's being sarcastic.*)

Bridget Well, everyone's going through a bad time at the moment. Everyone's feeling the pain.

Amanda Are they?

Bridget We are. I've had to look at all our ingoings and outgoings. I don't know if we'd be able to do this again. We've cut back on treats, discussed it with the children. We sat down . . .

Rory You sat down . . .

Bridget I sat down with the children and talked them through what has happened. The global financial crisis.

Amanda Bet that was fun.

Bridget They actually found it really interesting.

Rory Maybe the first ten minutes. They glazed over slightly when the PowerPoint presentation began.

Alan (*to Justine*) Shall we call it a night?

Bridget It's going to be an important part of our history. I think an understanding of economics is crucial to survival in this dog-eat-dog world and . . .

Alan didn't get a response. So he opens another drink.

Alistair Is there a point to where you're going with this?

Rory Probably not.

Bridget So, I went through their activities and told them they had to cut back on one of them. Said to Holly, you can have violin but not ballet as well. She was devastated. It's really tough.

Justine My heart bleeds.

Bridget I was just saying that we've found it difficult.

Alistair Everyone's finding it hard.

Bridget That's why we're all camping.

Alistair Exactly. Who's for a top-up?

He tries Justine's glass again.

Justine Still no.

Alistair Maybe we should call it a night?

Alistair signals to Amanda that they need to get rid of Bridget, Rory and Bronwyn. Behind their backs. She ignores him.

(*To Amanda, quiet to one side.*) Have you put the blockers on it? Again? I knew it . . .

Amanda Although this isn't our only holiday. We're going to the Maldives for our proper holiday next week. This was just an experiment.

Alan Oh, right.

Amanda Things have never been better, financially.

Alistair Darling . . .

Amanda And other friends in the City are still living the high life.

Alistair I know but . . .

Justine I never did catch what you did. You work in the City?

95

Alistair Well, yes . . .

Justine Right.

Alan (*trying to distract*) This is our last night. Let's just enjoy the food and talk about something lighter, shall we?

Amanda I know some people are really suffering, but others have never had it so good. A girlfriend of mine has this luxury candles business and she's never been so busy. Even through the supposed boom years, it was never as good as it is now. People spending hundreds of pounds at a time on candles in fancy boxes.

Justine Well, we're suffering. We've lost everything. We've got nothing to go back to. Our business has gone. Bust. Over. Our house is being repossessed while we're away. When we get back we move in with his parents.

Bronwyn hugs Justine.

Please don't be nice to me or I'll start crying again. Here we are in a pretend canvas house while our real one is being taken away from us.

Alan We're not talking about this here.

Justine I can't pretend any longer. Everything that defined us. Our house, our things, our success. All gone.

Rory But I thought . . . What about . . .?

Justine Oh no. The business is dead.

Bronwyn I'm so sorry.

Justine looks to Alan.

Alan It's out. Happy? Can we move on now?

Justine That's not it. You don't just say it and forget about it. It's like we're at different stages of grief. I don't know what's going on in his head. Even when we signed

96

all the bankruptcy papers he didn't react, didn't say anything. (*To Alan.*) What's going on? Say something. Do something. Are you going to react when we go back and we've got no house to go to?

Alan looks away and drinks his drink.

Bridget I think I've eaten enough. (*To Rory.*) Should we call it a . . .

Alistair This might be a bit brash, but was this really the best time to go on a fancy camping holiday?

Justine Yes, perhaps the stupidest idea in history.

Alistair If you can afford to come here –

Justine We'd already paid for it. Couldn't get the money back.

Bronwyn I'm so sorry. Hedge Funds Farms wouldn't let me.

Justine The kids needed a holiday. Why should they suffer? And we worked it out that they're taking the house back while we're here. So the kids wouldn't see any of it.

Alistair I suppose if your business was viable you'd still be afloat. That's how the market works.

Rory That's a bit insensitive.

Alan puts his head in his hands and starts to cry.

Amanda Oh dear.

Justine Don't cry – well, maybe do cry, it's good to cry.

Alan It's all my fault we're in this mess. My stupid dream to have my own business. To be somebody.

Justine You did your best.

Alan My best wasn't good enough. I should never have gone into business. And I should have protected the house, you, the kids.

Justine This is not your fault. This is bigger than you.

Alan Is it?

Bridget You're not the only one going through this. It's worldwide.

Alan Maybe I do need to let all this anger out.

Bridget Yes, good. You can't stay all bottled up, keeping it all in. It'll come out somewhere unexpected otherwise.

Alan I've got so much anger inside of me, that I keep a lid on. I'm scared to let it out. Because if I tap into it, who knows what will happen. (*To Justine.*) How should I let it all out? What do you suggest? You wanted a reaction. Here it is.

He punches Alistair in the face and sends him flying across the room.

Justine Alan!

Amanda What the . . .?

Rory Oh my God.

Bronwyn lets out a snort of laughter.

Bridget When I said let it out –

Alan How's that for starters?

He comes at Alistair again.

Alistair My teeth.

He punches Alistair.

The man's crazy.

Bridget I think we all need to calm down.

Justine Alan, what are you doing?

Alan grabs Alistair and gets him in a headlock.

Rory Now, Alan –

Bronwyn This is great!

Alistair Why me? This has nothing to do with me.

Alan Of course it was never going to work out for us. Set up a business, become your own boss. Play at being a grown-up. But for people like us it is just playing. It's all a lie. We're sold a story that's a lie.

Alistair coughs and splutters as Alan holds him tight.

Who'd have thought I'd have access to someone who created all this mess.

Alistair What? This has nothing to do with me.

Alan You work in the City. That's where this all started. It's because of twats like you that we're all in this mess.

Alistair What?

Amanda He's a dentist.

Alistair In the City. I have a practice in the City.

Amanda He's too thick to work with money, with numbers.

Alistair Can you just let me go now?

They all watch Alan. He doesn't move. He holds on to Alistair tightly.

Whatever's happened to you – this is not my doing.

Alan It's irrelevant what you do. It's who you are. And you're the nearest I'm ever going to get to anyone who's anything to do with this. This is as good as it gets.

Alistair Please let me go.

Alan How would you feel to be packing to go on holiday, all smiles and excitement for the kids, but you know you're never coming back to it?

Tears roll down Justine's cheeks.

Alistair I'm very sorry for you.

Alan Waving goodbye to their friends in the street. Telling them they'd see them in a week but they won't, because they're not coming back.

Alistair I understand.

Alan Do you? Would you ever understand?

Alistair Yes, please.

Bridget Will somebody please make him stop?

Amanda I'd be quite happy for you to finish him off.

Alistair Amanda, this is no time for jokes.

Amanda I'm deadly serious. I've had enough of you. All your games and 'It's just a little bit of fun'. I don't deserve to be treated like this. To be with someone like you.

Bridget Your children are just out there.

Alan thinks for a moment. It looks like he's about to let go of Alistair.

Bronwyn I sometimes think about walking through the village with a shotgun. Or going to find him and just blowing his face off. I know where you're coming from.

Alan grips Alistair's neck tighter. Alistair struggles and chokes.

Justine That wasn't very helpful.

Rory Actually, I could think of someone I'd like to shoot.

Alistair I'll do anything. I can give you some money. How much money do you want? I can write you a cheque.

Alan Are you serious? Do you think this is just about you having more money than me? And that you can buy yourself out of anything?

Amanda That's quite embarrassing, Alistair.

Alistair We're all friends together in this.

Alan How are we? Friends. People like you think you can have everything. That you can even have my wife.

Alan reaches across and grabs a knife out of the knife block and holds it at Alistair's throat.

Justine Alan!

Bridget Oh my God!

Rory Oh no.

Alan Do you think I'm stupid?

Justine Alan, please stop.

Alan (*to Justine*) I'm surprised you didn't go for it. Go for Mr Successful. Why would you want to be stuck with this failure? Eh? You want him? Have him.

Justine I'm sorry.

A sleepy Thomas, in his pyjamas, appears at the flap. He watches. No one else is aware.

Alan Have I really got anything to lose?

Justine Of course you have.

Alan I don't think I have.

Thomas Dad? What you doing?

Silence.

Dad?

Alan We're just playing a game, aren't we?

Alistair Yes, yes.

Thomas Why's Mum crying?

Justine It's all part of the game.

Thomas I don't like it. I don't like the game.

Alan puts the knife down and lets go of Alistair.

Alan Don't worry. We've finished the game now. Let's get you back to bed. Do you want to get in with me and Mum?

Thomas Can I? I thought we weren't allowed to do that any more?

Alan No, no. Of course you are.

Alan puts the knife to one side. He takes Thomas by the hand and leads him off through the flap and off to bed.
They all sit in silence.

Blackout.

SCENE TWO

Outside the front of the tent, a week later. The sun is shining brightly.
Justine stands looking out. Deep in thought.
Alan joins her from the right with a basket of logs and looks out. Pause.

Alan You okay?

Justine Yeah, yeah.

Pause.

Alan We're still here, then?

Justine I can't quite believe we're doing this.

Alan We don't have to.

Justine thinks.

It feels right . . . for now.

Justine Just for the summer holidays.

Alan One week at a time. See how we get on. It's rent-free.

Justine Yeah. Yeah.

Alan The kids love it. And it's a big enough house. And Bronwyn's off the dandelion wine. For now.

Justine That's a relief.

Alan She's cooking us a big stew tonight.

Justine (*still slightly distant*) Good.

Alan If it doesn't work out . . .

Justine Okay, okay. (*Pause.*) What else to do? First couple should be here soon.

Alan Got the logs ready for this one. It's a good workout, chopping wood.

He takes the wood inside the tent.

Justine Done the bedding in all three. Towels, candles . . . I think we're on top of everything.

Alan comes back out with a chicken in his arms.

Alan Look what I found in here. She must have just got in under the back.

He takes her off to one side.

Justine Is it Sheila? She's trouble, that one.

Alan comes back without the chicken.

Alan Go back up to your coop. Go on. You've done a great job. It looks perfect in there.

Justine Do you think we need to get anything else for the shop?

Alan No, stop worrying.

Justine I just want everything to be right.

Alan It is. There's nothing else for us to do now.

Justine Okay. (*Half to herself.*) Everything's okay.

They look out across the fields. Birds sing. Everything's okay for a moment. Justine puts her arm round Alan and gives him a kiss.

Alan What was that for?

Justine Shush.

A car horn beeps.

Alan They're here.

Justine I wonder what they're like? (*Shouting across.*) Look, kids, here's a new family coming. Do you want to go and greet them?

The sound of a car driving up. Justine and Alan look out over the countryside and take a deep breath.

Blackout.

End of play.